Francisco Mendoza Cervantes

A Problem-Oriented Approach for Dynamic Verification of Heterogeneous Embedded Systems

A Problem-Oriented Approach for Dynamic Verification of Heterogeneous Embedded Systems

by
Francisco Mendoza Cervantes

Dissertation, Karlsruher Institut für Technologie (KIT)
Fakultät für Elektrotechnik und Informationstechnik
Tag der mündlichen Prüfung: 15. Juli 2013
Referent: Prof. Dr.-Ing. Dr. h. c. Jürgen Becker
Korreferent: Prof. Dr.-Ing. Michael Hübner

Impressum

Scientific
Publishing

Karlsruher Institut für Technologie (KIT)
KIT Scientific Publishing
Straße am Forum 2
D-76131 Karlsruhe

KIT Scientific Publishing is a registered trademark of Karlsruhe
Institute of Technology. Reprint using the book cover is not allowed.

www.ksp.kit.edu

Print on Demand 2014

ISBN 978-3-7315-0169-5
DOI: 10.5445/KSP/1000038209

A Problem-Oriented Approach for Dynamic Verification of Heterogeneous Embedded Systems

Zur Erlangung des akademischen Grades eines

DOKTOR-INGENIEURS

von der Fakultät für
Elektrotechnik und Informationstechnik
des Karlsruher Instituts für Technologie (KIT)
genehmigte

DISSERTATION

von
M. Sc. Francisco Mendoza Cervantes
aus Mexiko Stadt

Hauptreferent:	Prof. Dr.-Ing. Dr. h. c. Jürgen Becker
Korreferent:	Prof. Dr.-Ing. Michael Hübner
Tag der mündlichen Prüfung:	15.07.2013

Februar 2014

Acknowledgments

The work presented ahead was carried out while I was working as a Research Scientist at the FZI Forschungszentrum Informatik in Karlsruhe. I would like to thank my former colleagues from the Embedded Systems and Sensors Engineering (ESS) group for their support and motivation. There are good memories and friendships from that time that I will always cherish.

There are also people from ABB Corporate Research that I would like to thank. Dr.-Ing. Philipp Nenninger for his trust and continuous support for my research. Dr.-Ing. Dirk John for believing in the benefits of this work in the industrial domain. Dr. Joris Pascal for providing an interesting industrial case study for this work and for his further collaboration on it. Finally, my colleagues from the Intelligent Devices group for their feedback on this work and for the multiple discussions regarding model based design approaches.

From the academic side, I want to thank my mentor and main advisor Prof. Dr.-Ing. Dr. h. c. Jürgen Becker for his support and for giving me the opportunity to carry out my research as part of the Karlsruhe Institute of Technology (KIT). Special thanks to Prof. Dr.-Ing. Michael Hübner for being co-advisor for this work and for supporting its application in the industrial domain.

My deepest appreciation goes to my family who provided me the determination to complete this dissertation. My parents for teaching me the values of honesty and hard work. My brother for always having an open ear for me. My wife for her love and patience, and for enduring the sleepless nights and weekends I invested in front of the computer. Without her none of this work would have been possible.

Abstract

Industrial devices in the industrial automation domain have undergone a steep increase in their complexity during the last 20 years. They have evolved from simple acquisition devices with point-to-point communication up to complex processing units with multiple computation and communication functionalities. This has given rise to a new series of design challenges for the embedded systems used to implement them.

Simulation based techniques are widely used for the design and verification of embedded systems for industrial devices. These systems are heterogeneous from a system level perspective due to the combination of digital systems, analog and mixed-signal systems and multi-domain physical systems. Various domain-specific modeling languages and simulation tools are available for this purpose. However, these tools focus on specific aspects of a design, which makes it very challenging to predict the behavior of full systems. This is done in late design stages, namely in the integration and tests phase, and often leads to time-consuming redesign cycles that affect the cost and time-to-market of a product.

This dissertation presents a virtual prototyping methodology for the design and verification of heterogeneous embedded systems. The targeted applications are industrial device such as sensor, actuators and close-loop controllers used to interact with physical processes in the field level of industrial automation systems. This methodology provides multidisciplinary team members with enhanced modeling and simulation capabilities in order to identify and solve design problems during early development stages. It also provides supporting modeling guidelines and a problem-oriented verification approach which can be applied in different development stages.

The virtual prototypes described in this work provide a pragmatic solution for emulating the behavior of hardware prototypes and experimental setups. The underlying simulation models used can be described in varying granularities according to the development stage, and using different modeling formalisms and simulation tools. This work demonstrates that virtual prototypes can help increase the confidence in the correctness of a design thanks to a deeper understanding of the complex interactions between hardware, software, analog and mixed-signal components of embedded systems and the physical processes they interact with.

Kurzfassung

Industrielle Geräte in der Automatisierungstechnik sind in den letzten 20 Jahren deutlich komplexer geworden. Sie haben sich von einfachen Messgeräten mit Punkt-zu-Punkt Kommunikation zu Einheiten mit mehreren Kommunikations- und Verarbeitungsfunktionen entwickelt. Ihre zunehmende Komplexität führt zu neuen Herausforderungen in der Entwicklung derartiger eingebetteter Systeme.

Diese eingebetteten Systeme werden auf Systemebene als heterogen bezeichnet, da digitale, analoge und mixed-Signal Komponenten mit Multidomain-physikalischen Systemen zusammenwirken. Zur Entwicklung und Verifikation solcher Systeme werden häufig simulationsbasierte Verfahren eingesetzt. Diese Verfahren erfolgen durch mehrere domain-spezifische Modellierungssprachen und Werkzeuge, die auf spezifischen Teilen des Systems ausgerichtet sind. Das Gesamtverhalten kann daher erst in einer späteren Entwicklungsphase, nämlich der Integrationsphase, getestet werden. Dabei kommt es oft zu zeitaufwendigen Redesign-Zyklen, die sich auf Kosten und time-to-market eines Produkts auswirken.

In dieser Dissertation wird eine auf Virtual Prototyping basierende Vorgehensweise für die Entwicklung und Verifikation heterogener eingebetteter Systeme vorgeschlagen. Gezielte Anwendungen sind industrielle Geräte wie Sensoren, Aktoren und Regler, die mit physikalischen Prozessen auf der Feldebene von industriellen Automatisierungssystemen zusammenwirken. Die entwickelte Methode gibt multidisziplinären Arbeitsgruppen verbesserte Modellierungs- und Simulationsfähigkeiten zur Identifizierung und Lösung von Entwicklungsproblemen in frühen Entwicklungsphasen an die Hand. Dabei werden auch Modellierungsrichtlinien und ein problem-basiertes Verifikationsverfahren, welches in verschiedenen Entwicklungsphasen anwendbar ist, beschrieben.

Die in dieser Arbeit dargestellten virtuellen Prototypen bieten eine pragmatische Lösung für die Simulation von Hardwareprototypen und Testaufbauten. Die zugrunde liegenden Simulationsmodelle werden, entsprechend der Entwicklungsphase, mit verschiedenen Modellierungssprachen in variierendem Detaillierungsgrad beschrieben. Diese Arbeit zeigt, dass virtuelle Prototypen das Vertrauen in die Richtigkeit eines Designs stärken können, da sie zu einem tieferen Verständnis für die Wechselwirkungen zwischen der Komponenten von heterogenen eingebetteten Systemen und den physikalischen Systemen, mit denen sie zusammenwirken, führen.

Contents

1

Introduction

1.1 Industrial devices in automation systems

The day-to-day operations of most production and manufacturing plants are possible thanks to industrial automation systems. They form part of many industry sectors, including chemical and petrochemical, food and beverage, pulp and paper, oil and gas, power generation, mining, among many others. Their goal is to make production processes more efficient, cost effective and fast enough to keep up with market demands.

The primary activities performed by industrial automation systems are the monitoring and control of industrial processes. A wide range of industrial devices, interconnected by industrial networks and field buses, are used for this purpose. Figure 1.1 illustrates a typical example in the process automation domain. It also shows the different levels of an industrial automation system and its interconnection topology. The station level is responsible for monitoring and process optimization tasks, the control level is responsible, as its name specifies, for control tasks, and the field level is responsible for sensing and actuation tasks. This clear separation of tasks, in hand with available means for sharing information between them, makes it possible to automate even the most complex industrial processes.

Industrial devices, also called industrial instruments or field devices, are highly reliable and robust sensors, actuators and controllers located in the field level of industrial automation systems. Some examples in the process automation domain are illustrated

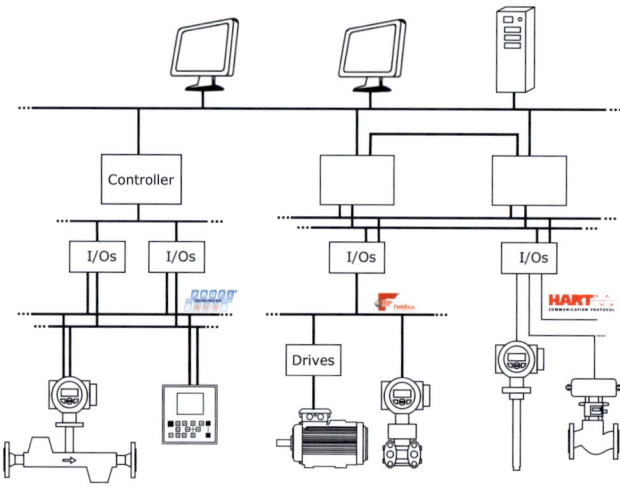

Figure 1.1: Industrial automation system

in the bottom part of Figure 1.1. They are sensing devices such as temperature sensors, flow sensors and pressure sensors. They are also actuators such as valves and motor drives, as well as local controllers such as industrial PID controllers. Another example from a different application domain are IEDs (Intelligent Electronic Devices) used in power systems. They are highly complex sensing devices for electric measurements and are used in electrical substations for monitoring and protection purposes. All these devices act as the eyes and hands of higher level control and monitoring systems. Their communication with upper levels of automation networks is implemented by a variety of field buses and communication protocols.

1.2 Design challenges for industrial devices

During the last 20 years, the amount of computation and communication functionalities embedded into industrial devices has considerably increased [100]. Figure 1.2 helps to illustrate the evolution of industrial devices during this time. Devices that where once point-to-point transmitters of process variables are now intelligent devices capable of performing multiple additional functionalities. For instance, they are equipped with advanced signal processing capabilities, they perform multiple self-diagnostic function-alities, they perform distributed control functions and they are able to communicate independently with other devices.

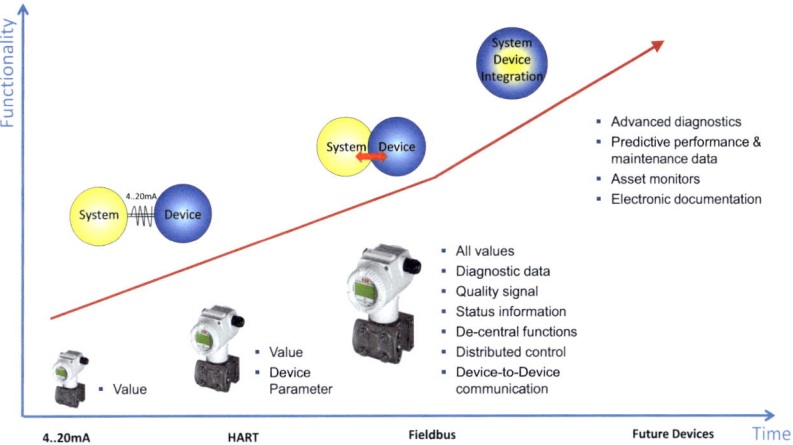

Figure 1.2: Increasing functionality of industrial devices

The design of embedded systems for industrial devices is a multidisciplinary activity that requires domain experts on digital and physical aspects of a design. Digital aspects refer to hardware and software components. Meanwhile, physical aspects refer to the physics behind the plant or process involved, as well as the analog and mixed-signal components used to interact with it. This combination of digital, mixed-signal, analog and physical systems lead to their classification as heterogeneous embedded system.

Certain assumptions must be done to separate digital and physical aspects of a design. The purpose of this separation is to reduce the complexity of a system by breaking it down into smaller and more manageable parts. For instance, a common approach in HW/SW (Hardware/Software) co-design of digital systems is the use of test benches. A common simplification is to consider test benches as static elements, such as sinks and sources. This is not valid when the execution of HW/SW components being developed is dependent on the behavior of physical processes they interact with. Physical processes are dynamic systems sensitive to a number of factors, such as feedback control, disturbances and particular operation points. Ignoring the intrinsic dynamic characteristics of physical processes in test benches is commonly a reason for integration problems that happen in later design stages. This results in unforeseen interactions between physical processes and components of embedded systems that can lead to costly and time-consuming redesign cycles.

A similar premise is used by authors such as *Branicky* [23] for describing hybrid systems, as well as *Lee* [82] and *Karsai* [75] for describing CPS (Cyber-Physical Systems). Their premise states that from a system level perspective, the execution of computation

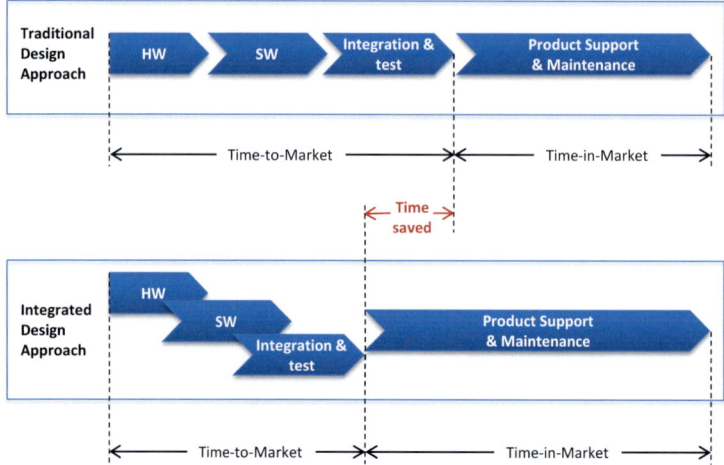

Figure 1.3: Example of an integrated design approach for embedded systems

and communication tasks performed by an embedded system are directly affected by the behavior of the physical process it interacts with and vice versa.

Industrial devices evidently fall into the classification of hybrid or cyber-physical systems since heterogeneous embedded systems are used for the measurement and control of physical processes. Similar examples can be found in other industries such as automotive, avionics, medicine technology, etc. The design challenges are to ensure the predictability and reliability of such systems, while at the same time keeping up with constraining time-to-market requirements. These challenges arise when digital and physical domains are closely coupled.

The assumptions made on early design stages due to the partitioning and simplification of digital and physical domains may not always be valid. They lead to inconsistencies in the specifications by which embedded systems are designed. The result is an increased number of iterative redesign cycles, which consequently leads to long times-to-market and costly development processes.

An improved design approach is needed. This is exemplary illustrated in Figure 1.3. It is an integrated design approach that envisions design teams working in parallel and being able to share and test their results together at different design stages. The advantage with respect to traditional design approaches is the possibility to perform verification and validation of complete systems at different designs stages. Higher quality results, in a shorter time-to-market, can be obtained thanks to the identification and resolution of design errors in earlier design stages.

In practice, an ideal design flow such as the one illustrated in Figure 1.3 does not exist. Many technical tradeoffs must be considered, for example, the type of embedded systems being designed, their complexity, and the tools and modeling formalisms used. External factors must also be considered, such as the acceptance of development teams to adopt new design approaches and the overhead that this might bring.

1.3 Goals of this work

Traditional design approaches for embedded systems are characterized by their dependency on hardware prototypes and experimental setups for verification and validation purposes. More recent approaches such as Rapid Prototyping and Hardware-in-the-Loop testing are available that can help make this verification and validation process more reliable and efficient. A third and more recent approach is Virtual Prototyping. Virtual prototyping stands for the verification and validation of embedded systems using system level simulation models that emulate (mimic) the behavior of hardware prototypes and experimental setups.

Simulation techniques are an established aid during the development of embedded systems. They are used by various domains experts (hardware engineers, embedded software developers, physicist, etc.) for understanding and designing particular parts of a system. However, the impact of crossing simulation boundaries is rarely considered. Virtual prototypes offer the possibility to bridge the simulation boundaries between digital, analog and physical domains in order to have a better understanding of the systems being developed and of the complex interactions among them.

Related work on virtual prototyping include Ptolemy II [38, 44], the CODIS co-simulation framework [21, 51], the work from *Kirchner et al.* [77, 78] and the dissertation from *Verhoef* [134]. In these, the following points have not been fully addressed:

- The use of virtual prototypes for supporting various stages of the development life-cycle of heterogeneous embedded systems have not been investigated

- The possibility to reuse and test existing device firmware inside virtual prototypes has not been considered. This includes embedded legacy code and hardware dependent software (drivers and real time operating systems).

- The simulation of overall systems, which includes digital and physical domains, using processor emulation tools has not been addressed until now

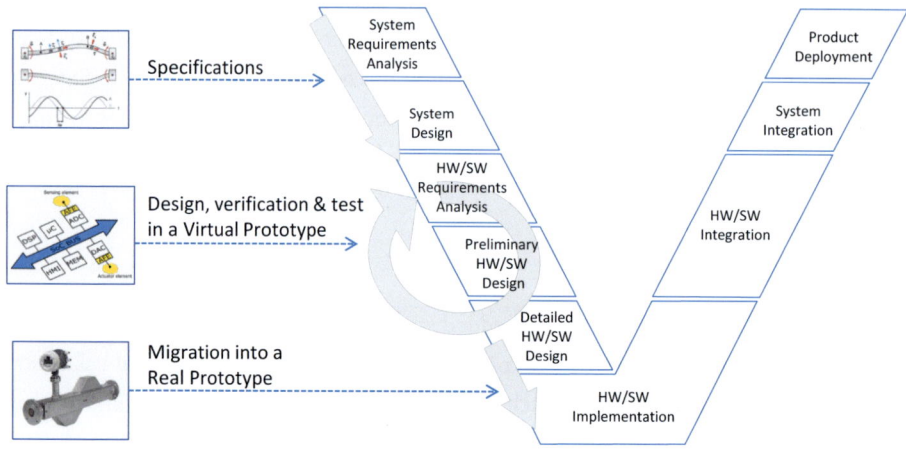

Figure 1.4: Virtual prototyping in the design of industrial devices

These points and their appropriate solutions will be addressed in this dissertation. This work proposes a virtual prototyping methodology for the design and verification of heterogeneous embedded systems. Its role in the design flow of industrial devices is illustrated in Figure 1.4. It is a model-based design approach that brings together hardware, software, analog and mixed-signal component models of embedded systems with physical models of their environment. It enables a new dimension of testing and verification capabilities by considering the effects that functional, structural and physical specifications have in the behavior of full systems. It also speeds up the design process since iterative design cycles are performed in a virtual environment, which is much faster than with real hardware prototypes and experimental setups.

The goal of this dissertation is to enable the use of overall system simulation approaches throughout the development process of heterogeneous embedded systems for industrial devices and to provide a supporting methodology for it. This work is intended to provide multidisciplinary team members with enhanced verification capabilities to identify and solve design problems during early development stages. This is possible by coupling the execution of different simulators, each one responsible for obtaining the behavior of part of a system. The combined execution of simulators can help increase the understanding of interdependencies between different system components. This eventually helps increase the confidence in the correctness of a design, thereby reducing risks in a project and leading to hardware prototypes and experimental setups that are built right the first time. Thereby, the following points will be addressed in this work:

1. *A multi-domain simulation framework* where digital and physical system level models can interact in a correct and reproducible manner. The selected tools and modeling formalisms must be compatible with best-practices used in the industrial automation domain.

2. *A set of modeling guidelines* intended to decrease the implementation effort of the proposed design methodology. The guidelines must provide a set of rules for the construction of consistent and meaningful virtual prototypes. They should ease the creation of virtual prototypes and help increase the reusability of designs.

3. *A problem-oriented verification methodology* for identifying and solving design problems before they propagate into further development stages. It should allow for top-down or bottom-up verification approaches in order to target specific verification goals. This should help increase the confidence in the correctness of heterogeneous embedded system designs.

1.4 Outline of this work

Chapter 2 gives an overview of the applications of industrial devices, their embedded systems and some of the best-practices used during their design. The initial requirements are identified and used as driving force for the work presented in the following chapters.

Chapter 3 and Chapter 4 describe the state-of-the-art on model based design approaches for heterogeneous embedded systems. This includes approaches for describing digital systems, analog and mixed-signal systems and physical systems. The state-of-the-art is evaluated regarding requirement for the design of industrial devices in order to define the scope of this dissertation.

Chapter 5 and Chapter 6 describe the proposed virtual prototyping methodology for the design, verification and test of industrial devices. These chapters define modeling guidelines for creating virtual prototypes and a problem-oriented verification methodology applicable to different design stages.

Chapter 7 describes a multi-domain simulation framework that enables the verification strategies of the above-mentioned virtual prototypes. It describes a generic and efficient co-simulation algorithm for coupling continuous-time and discrete-event simulators. It also describes its implementation for coupling SystemC/Simulink and SystemC/VHDL-AMS simulation engines.

Chapter 8 describes the evaluation of the work presented in this dissertation. Two application examples are presented: the first one is based on an academic example and the second on an ongoing industrial project.

Chapter 9 presents the conclusions of this work and an outlook for further research on applications for virtual prototyping methodologies in the industrial automation domain.

2

Industrial Devices

This chapter provides the necessary background for understanding the challenges encountered during the design of industrial devices used in the field level of industrial automation systems. These devices are complex heterogeneous embedded systems responsible for the monitoring, measurement and manipulation of physical processes in the field level. This chapter gives an overview of the applications of industrial devices, their embedded systems and some of the best-practices used during their design. The initial requirements for this dissertation are identified and are used as driving force for the work presented in the following chapters.

2.1 Industrial devices in automation systems

The overall goal of industrial automation systems is to optimize processes and assets in all levels of an organization. This is archived by various electronic systems that gather information from physical processes in order to control them in a safe, reliable and efficient manner. Industrial automation systems can be found in any major industrial sector. Some examples are listed in Table 2.1.

Industrial automation systems are distributed across all layers of an organization as shown in Figure 2.1. This helps identify the different levels of an industrial automation system, as well as the main activities performed in each of them. Since the scope of this dissertation is on industrial devices on the field level, only the three bottom levels of

Sector	Industries
Power generation	coal, gas, wind, solar
Distribution	water, gas, oil, electricity
Process manufacturing	food & beverage, chemical, pharmaceutical
Discrete manufacturing	automotive, electronic appliances
Buildings	HVAC, lighting
Transportation	railways, maritime ports, airports

Table 2.1: Example of industries relying on industrial automation systems

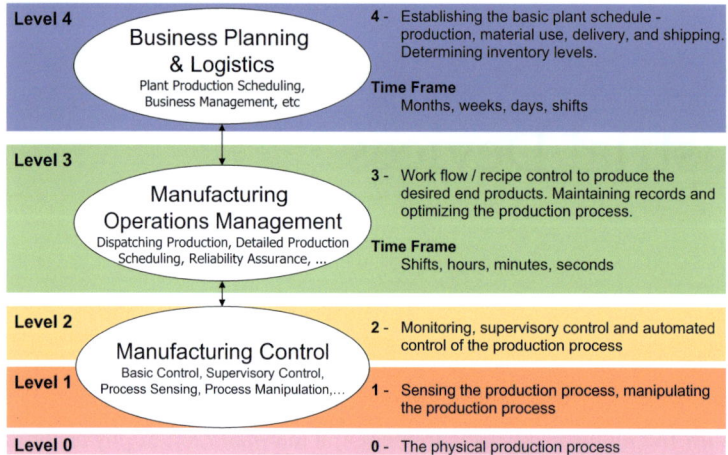

Figure 2.1: Hierarchy of industrial automation system according to ISA-95 [19]

Figure 2.1, corresponding to manufacturing control activities, will be described ahead.

2.1.1 Industrial processes

This section describes in more detail the physical production processes corresponding to Level-0 of Figure 2.1. According to the DIN19222 [39] control technology terminology, a process is defined as a set of concurrent operations acting upon a system in which mater, energy or information is transformed, transported or stored. The definition applies to any type of industrial process, e.g. a petrochemical process in a refinery plant or an assembly process in the automotive industry. Moreover, the ISA-95 standard [74] further classifies processes into three types: continuous, discrete and batch processes.

Continuous processes

Continuous processes are associated with the transformation of raw materials into products. The transformation process results in a product that cannot be separated into its raw materials, e.g. oil refinement, electricity generation, food and beverage products. Such systems require sensors and actuators that determine and regulate physical properties of raw materials, and control systems that monitor and control the overall transformation process. Continuous control systems are used extensively in industrial applications such as: food & beverage, pulp & paper, oil & gas, chemical processing, power generation and distribution, etc.

From a mathematical point of view, the behavior of continuous processes is described by continuous states and state transitions. They are monotone and reversible [95], which makes them controllable by techniques such as feedback control. Thereby, control tasks for continuous processes focus mainly on the regulation of measurable physical properties.

Discrete processes

Discrete processes are associated with the assembly of parts into a final product. The transformation process is reversible, thus individual parts can be identified in the final product. Such systems require sensors and actuators that can determine and alter the state of a system according to commands from a control system. Discrete control systems are used extensively in the automotive industry, for example, to assemble parts in a car and to transport it to different locations inside a plant. Many industries rely on discrete control systems for activities such as printing, sorting, packing and transport of materials or products via conveyor belts or cranes.

From a mathematical point of view, the behavior of discrete processes is described by discrete states and abrupt state transitions from one state to the next caused by input events. They are reversible and not monotone [95], meaning that the removal of an input stimuli will not necessarily bring a process back to its previous state. Thereby, control tasks for discrete processes focus mainly on the calculation of discrete sets of commands that can bring a process to a desired state.

Batch processes

Batch processes are systems with continuous and discrete processes. Pharmaceutical and chemical industries are classical examples of applications with dominantly batch processes. In this context, a control task is represented by a sequence of discrete steps needed to carry out a recipe, while each step is described by a continuous process particular to the assigned resource (e.g. heating, filling, mixing). For example, in a bottle-filling application a discrete process describes the sequence of events for bottles transported on a conveyor belt, while a continuous process describes the filling process (pour a certain volume of liquid into each bottle).

2.1.2 Industrial devices

This section describes in more detail the industrial devices used for sensing and manipulation activities corresponding to Level-1 of Figure 2.1. Industrial devices are highly specialized electronic devices responsible for the measurement and control of industrial processes. They are further classified as discrete and continuous instruments, according to the type of industrial processes they interact with.

Discrete instruments

Discrete instrumentation devices are sensors and actuators used to identify and manipulate discrete states of a process. Examples of such devices are proximity detectors. They are micro-switches, optical sensors or magnetic sensors that communicate binary values about the presence or absence of an object. Further examples are pushbuttons, position encoders and identification solutions (bar code scanners, RFID detectors, machine vision, etc.).

Continuous instruments

Instrumentation devices for continuous processes are responsible for the measurement, manipulation and local control of continuous processes. Figure 2.2 shows classical examples of industrial devices for continuous process in the process automation market. They correspond to one of the categories listed below:

- *Sensors.-* Measurement devices that extract process variables and transmit them to control and automation systems. Such variables are related to physical properties of a system, thereby requiring specialized sensing elements and measurement principles. Some examples are sensors for temperature, pressure, flow and level.

- *Actuators.-* Responsible for executing manipulation tasks coming from control and automation systems. Some examples of actuators in industrial applications are electric contactors, heating elements, pneumatic and hydraulic positioners and electric motors.

- *Recorders and controllers.-* They provide data visualization and control capabilities of continuous processes. They are installed directly in the field level, in proximity with sensing devices and actuators. The most common example are PID process controllers.

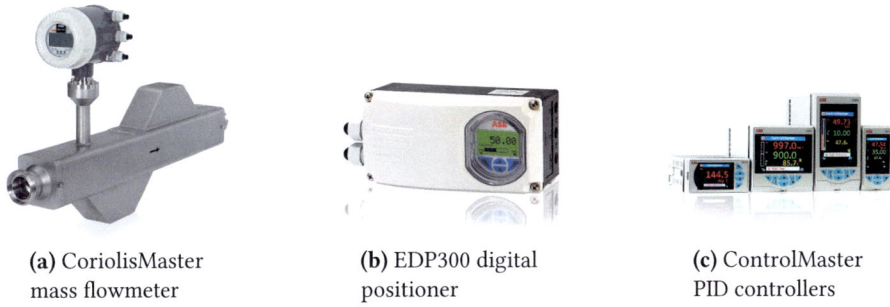

(a) CoriolisMaster
mass flowmeter

(b) EDP300 digital
positioner

(c) ControlMaster
PID controllers

Figure 2.2: Examples of continuous instruments offered by ABB

2.1.3 Industrial controllers

This section describes in more detail the industrial controllers used for monitoring, supervision and control activities corresponding to Level-3 of Figure 2.1. The distinction between continuous, discrete and batch processes has led to the specialization of industrial automation systems. Figure 2.3 illustrates the classification of industrial automation systems according to the type of process they interact with. Each market specializes on specific type of processes: factory automation on discrete processes, hybrid automation on batch processes and process automation on continuous processes. It is also interesting to notice that not only the type of processes determines the most adequate control system, but also the size and complexity of a process.

In the factory automation market, monitoring and control tasks are carried out by the combination of SCADA (Supervisory Control and Data Acquisition) systems and PLC (Programmable Logic Controller) systems. PLC controllers are affordable industrial controllers specializing on medium to low complexity tasks related with discrete processes. Various PLC controllers may be utilized in a plant according to its size and control requirements. An example of a PLC controller, the AC500 from ABB, is presented in Figure 2.4a. SCADA systems provide an overview of the control operations carried out by PLC controllers. Their task is the supervision and collection of all data coming from PLC controllers. Often, they are accompanied with data visualization solutions useful to present the state of a process in real-time.

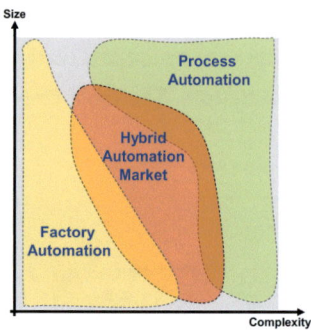

Figure 2.3: Classification of markets for industrial automation systems [3]

In the process automation market, monitoring, data acquisition and control tasks are carried out by DCS (Distributed Control Systems) systems. DCS systems are more complex than their SCADA/PLC counterparts in factory automation. In comparison to SCADA/PLC combinations, DCS systems centralize distributed control operations, provide advanced functionalities and can handle more I/O modules. Another difference to SCADA/PLC combinations is that DCS systems provide diagnosis information of processes and enable remote access to field devices from an operator console. This is possible thanks to more intelligent field devices and more advanced communication protocols. The application market of DCS control systems are plants with complex continuous and batch processes. An example of a DCS controller is the 800M controller from ABB showed in Figure 2.4c.

The hybrid automation market offers monitoring and control solutions for continuous/discrete and batch processes of middle complexity. Such solutions may include SCADA/PLC and DCS combinations or dedicated systems such as the Freelance controller from ABB showed in Figure 2.4b.

(a) AC500 PLC   **(b)** 800F Freelance   **(c)** 800M DCS

Figure 2.4: Examples of industrial automation systems offered by ABB

2.1.4 Industrial communication

The communication requirements for each level of an automation system are very different. For instance, at the field level hundreds or thousands of instruments communicate data via dedicated lines or shared fieldbuses. This requires robust communication networks with various data rates and real-time constraints. Data is then gathered in the control level where new commands are issued. This requires communication networks that support high data rates and real-time constraints. Finally, communication networks in the station level have even higher data rates, but no real-time constraints since mainly monitoring activities are performed.

Various communication standards are available in the industrial automation domain. Some of the most significant industrial communication standards are listed in Table 2.2. The most relevant of these are described ahead.

4-20mA

The simplest industrial communication standard available is the 4-20mA hardwire communication. It has been used for decades in the process automation market and is still widely implemented. It enables the transmission of primary process variables encoded as a 4-20mA analog current. Basic error signalization is possible by transmitting current values on defined ranges outside the 4-20mA range [43]. The physical mediums are point-to-point 2-wire or 4-wire cables between field devices and I/O modules of a controller. This creates a current loop for the transmission of analog data. The key elements of current loops are analog transmitters. These can be sensing elements, such as temperature transmitters, or I/Os from a controller. The advantage of 4-20mA current loops is that they provide a simple and robust communication medium for transferring analog data. Since the information is an electrical current value, it is insensitive to the line resistance or voltage variations. The disadvantages are the amount of cabling required for their installation, the limited amount of information that can be transferred (only

Field Level	4-20mA, HART, FOUNDATION Fieldbus, Profibus DP/PA, PROFINET IO, Modbus RTU, CANopen, IEC 61850-9-2
Control Level	FOUNDATION Fieldbus, PROFINET, Modbus TCP, IEC 61850-8
Station Level	Ethernet TCP/IP

Table 2.2: Examples of industrial communication networks

one process variable), and that the communication is unidirectional (sensor-controller or controller-actuator).

HART

The HART (Highway Addressable Remote Transducer) industrial communication protocol is widely used in the process automation market. It is backwards compatible with 4-20mA communication standard in order to reuse available cabling from existing installations. The HART communication protocol uses a frequency shift keying principle to modulate digital signals onto a 4-20 mA DC analog current [58]. Physical connections between field devices and I/Os of controllers can be point-to-point or multi-drop. In point-to-point connections, primary process variables are transmitted as analog currents and secondary process variables from intelligent field devices are transmitted as modulated digital signals. In multi-drop connections, multiple field devices can be connected to the same current loop. Since all devices share the same physical medium, primary and secondary process variables from intelligent field devices are transmitted digitally upon polling requests from a controller.

Fieldbuses

A variety of fieldbus communication standards from different standardization organizations are available. In the factory automation market, simple fieldbuses are required since the data transferred are discrete values. Examples of fieldbuses with low overhead and small data packets are Seriplex, Interbus-S, and AS-I (AS-Interface), which are sometimes called sensor buses or bit level buses [16]. Other more advanced fieldbuses are DeviceNet, ControlNet, and PROFIBUS DP, which are referred to as device buses or byte-level buses [16].

In the process automation market, digital communication protocols such as FOUNDATION Fieldbus and Profibus are widely used. In comparison to HART, they are fully digital and are not backwards compatible with 4-20mA installations. Instead, they rely on a bus topology where instrumentation devices and controllers are connected to.

The substation automation market uses industrial communication standards which are similar to fieldbuses in the process automation market. Since 2002, various device manufacturers have started to follow a new Ethernet-based communication standard called IEC 61850 [22]. The IEC 61850 solves interoperability problems between devices developed by different manufacturers and enables the use of more intelligent devices called IEDs (Intelligent Electronic Devices). They are used for protection, control and

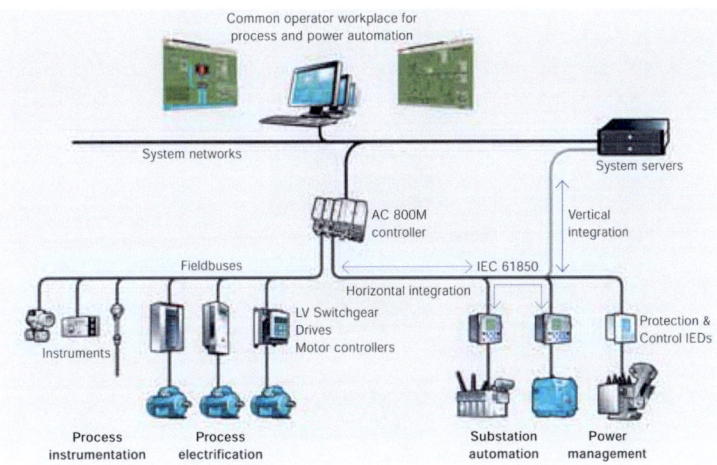

Figure 2.5: Integrated process and power automation [56]

electrical metering. They connect to instrument transformers and primary equipment in switchyards, such as switchgear and power transformers. IEDs are similar in terms of computation and communication capabilities to field devices in the process automation market. Figure 2.5 shows an example of how fieldbuses for process automation and the IEC 61850 for substation automation are able to coexist in a plant thanks to advanced DCS control systems.

2.2 Embedded systems for industrial devices

Each level of an industrial automation system relies on different underlying technologies. They are selected according to requirements such as processing power, memory, communication data rates and real-time behavior. For instance, in the station level, tasks are highly data oriented. Large amounts of information, generated by the control and field levels, need to be stored, transferred and monitored. The underlying technologies are typically general purpose, such as PCs, data servers and high bandwidth networks. In the case of the control level, multiple industrial processes, sometimes strictly dependent on each other, need to be carefully orchestrated and synchronized. This requires the execution of multiple control cycles with real-time processing and communication constraints. The underlying technologies are industrial computers relying on powerful processor architectures, as well as various types of industrial networks. Lastly, in the field level, highly specialized sensing, manipulation and local control tasks need to be

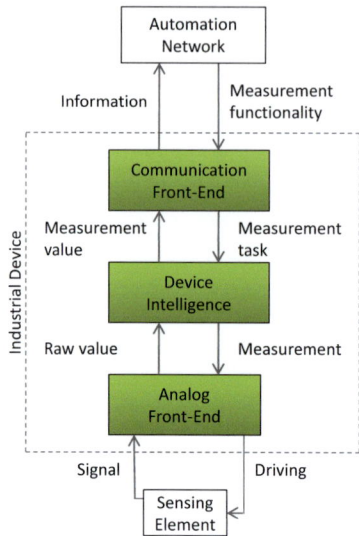

Figure 2.6: Basic structure and functionality of an industrial measurement device

performed. Real-time processing and communication constraints apply here as well. The underlying technologies are embedded systems with strict limitations regarding their processing and communication capabilities, memory and power consumption.

Figure 2.6 shows the basic structure and functionality of an industrial measurement device. It relies on three main components for its operation: an analog front-end, a device intelligence module and a communication front-end. The analog front-end is responsible for interacting with transducers and other sensing/actuating elements. It performs function such as signal adaption, filtering and quantization. The device intelligence is responsible for the execution of measurement tasks and for performing data analysis on acquired data sets. It may also be responsible for the execution of communication stacks. Finally, the communication front-end is responsible for the communication with higher levels of an automation system using industrial communication standards such as 4-20mA, HART or some digital fieldbus.

The structure and functionality of modern industrial devices is in reality more complex. In general, they all rely on the three basic modules explained above (analog front-end, device intelligence and communication front-end). However, each of these modules must be tailored according to particular applications and requirements. They also support a number of additional functionalities which are constantly evolving in new product lines. Such increase in functionality is intended to provide a better handling of industrial devices themselves (e.g. useful during commissioning, maintenance, diagnosis) and to make the operation of an industrial automation system more efficient (e.g. higher accuracy, better transient response, lower power consumption).

2.2.1 Hardware platforms

Industrial devices are designed for particular measurement and control applications. They are also designed according to particular hardware safety requirements such as SIL (Safety Integrity Level) certification and explosion safety protection. Therefore, the complexity and heterogeneity of hardware platforms for industrial devices can vary significantly. They may include a variety of software programmable components (e.g. microcontrollers, DSPs, hard/soft cores in FPGAs), hardware programmable components (e.g. FPGAs), digital and mixed-signal off-the-shelf components (e.g. memories, A/D and D/A converters, transceivers) and analog circuitry (e.g. protection circuits, filters, multiplexers, voltage regulators, transducers).

Figure 2.7 shows an example of a hardware platform of an industrial temperature transmitter. It is a 2-wire platform, where a device is powered by the same two wires used for 4-20mA communication. The block diagram shows in a simplified way the digital, analog and mixed-signal components that make up its structure. The analog front-end is implemented by analog and mixed-signal components such as analog filters, a multiplexer, an A/D converter and other analog circuitry. The device intelligence is implemented by digital components, in this case two microcontrollers due to the galvanic isolation between circuitry on the process side and circuitry on the automation network side. The communication front-end is implemented by further mixed-signal components such as a voltage-to-current converter, a D/A converter and a frequency shift keying signal modulator for HART communication. In this example, a typical distribution of tasks are signal adaption and sensing tasks in the in the left side of the galvanic isolation, whereas signal processing and communication tasks are assigned to the right side of the galvanic isolation.

2.2.2 Device firmware

The device firmware of an industrial device is composed of hardware-dependent and hardware-independent software components as illustrated in Figure 2.8. Hardware dependent software is shown in the bottom part of Figure 2.8 and includes boot firmware, device drivers, communication protocol stacks and real-time operating systems. Hardware independent software, or simply software as depicted in the top part of Figure 2.8, includes middleware, adapters and subsystems for application software.

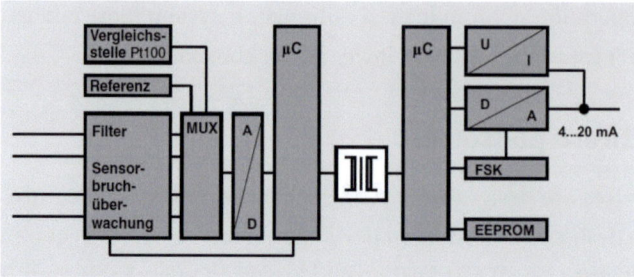

Figure 2.7: Block diagram of an industrial temperature transmitter circuitry[43]

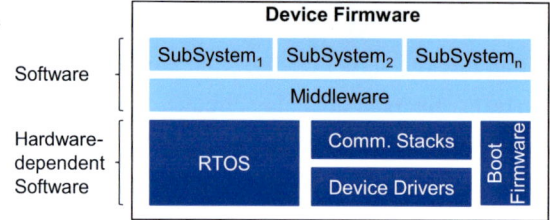

Figure 2.8: Device firmware of an industrial device

Software is the primary mean for implementing communication and computation functionalities in industrial devices. Application software is encapsulated in subsystems derived from component based approaches [100]. In component based approaches, subsystems are defined as sets of related functions and data objects that are able to communicate with each other through well-known interfaces. This is vital for maintaining software architectures of industrials devices and for reusing software components throughout different product line.

2.3 Design approaches for industrial devices

Figure 2.9 illustrates the initial stages of the design of embedded systems for industrial devices. It corresponds to the left side of the V-Model. A similar design flow is followed in most applications where embedded systems are used to interact with physical processes. It starts with the definition of the system specifications and ends with the creation of a hardware prototype and an experimental setup. Further steps in the design include integration and testing phases, corresponding to the right side of the V-Model, and are not shown in the figure.

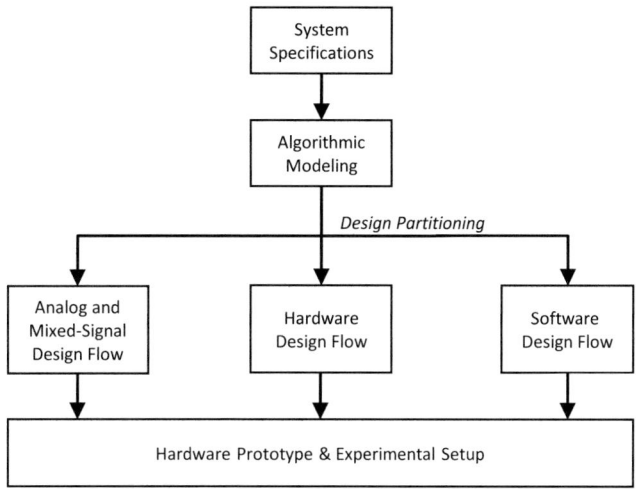

Figure 2.9: Design flow of embedded systems

System specifications are based on functional and non-functional requirements. Functional requirements describe the particular measurement or control principles that need to be implemented in an embedded system, as well as boundary conditions for its operation. Non-functional requirements include things like operation temperature range, safety considerations, robustness considerations, the desired power consumption, footprint and cost, etc.

Algorithmic models are derived from functional system specifications. They are behavioral models described using formalisms such as mathematical equations, lumped models or transfer functions. Within the algorithmic modeling stage, measurement and control algorithms, which will be later executed in an embedded system, are verified and validated together with plant models. Commercial modeling and simulation tools for dynamic systems such as MATLAB /Simulink and LabVIEW are commonly used during this stage. Further examples are multi-body system dynamics simulation tools such as Modelica, ADAMS, RecurDyn or Simpack.

Once enough knowledge of a system's behavior has been gathered during the algorithm modeling phase, a complete paradigm shift occurs. This is depicted in Figure 2.9 as design partitioning. It refers to the partitioning of embedded system functionality into hardware, software, analog and mixed-signal components. Afterwards, each of them is independently designed using specialized tools and formalisms. These are, for instance, software compilers and debuggers for the software design flow, synthesis and place-and-route tools for the hardware design flow, and circuit schematics tools for the analog design flow.

Hardware, software, analog and mixed-signal components of a system are brought together in the integration phase for the construction of a first hardware prototype. Experimental setups are also constructed in test laboratories equipped with appropriate test equipment. For instance, a typical test setup for a flow meter requires test labs equipped with water tanks, pipes, heaters, pumps, etc. Within this stage, design iterations on hardware prototypes must be performed to correct possible design errors. This results in the creation of further versions of hardware prototypes and may involve performing changes in experimental setups. Solving design problems in such late design stages implies costly and time consuming redesign cycles that may take months to complete. This can severely increase a project's risk, delaying times-to-market and increasing the overall cost of a project.

2.4 Identification of requirements for this work

During the design of industrial devices, a considerable amount of time and effort is invested in the integration phase. Within this phase, the identification of design errors typically means going back to previous design stages and, in some cases, performing subsequent redesign of a hardware prototype. The reasons of such problems include:

- Inconsistencies in the specifications

- Misunderstanding of specifications by different team members

- Lack of specification follow-up throughout the design phase

- Unexpected interactions between internal components of embedded systems

- Unexpected interactions between components of embedded system and their physical environment

Virtual prototypes make it possible to identify and correct the problems listed above using overall system level simulations. Such problems might otherwise appear in later design stages, where the cost of solving them increases. Overall system level simulation refer to the combined simulation of hardware, software, analog and mixed-signal components of embedded systems together with physical models of the plants or processes they interact with. A methodology is required that can help guide the generation of such virtual prototypes and their subsequent use for the resolution of possible design problems.

Simulation techniques are extensively used during the design of industrial devices. They are highly specialized, thereby used for the design of particular parts of a system, which can be hardware, software, analog or mixed-signal components. Overall simulations are possible by bringing together different parts of a system and their respective simulation engines. This is not a trivial task and requires a deep understanding of the models of computation behind each simulation engine. Therefore, the following issues have been identified and will be addressed in this dissertation:

1. How to describe the structure and behavior of embedded systems (including hardware, software, analog and mixed signal components) and the physical models of their environment?

2. Which information is necessary for the creation of meaningful models of embedded systems and their environment and at what point of the development process are they available?

3. Which problems can be addressed by overall system level simulation of embedded systems and physical models and at what stages of the development process can they be used?

4. How can overall system level simulation approaches be integrated into existing development processes of industrial devices?

Point 1 is addressed in Chapter 3 and Chapter 4 with appropriate models of computation for describing and simulating embedded system components and physical processes. Point 2 is addressed in Chapter 5 with modeling guidelines that define the amount of detail permitted in a model and define how simulation results must be accordingly interpreted. Point 3 is addressed in Chapter 6 with a problem-oriented design methodology that correlates the type of models that must be used according to particular problems that need to be solved during different design stages. Point 4 is addressed in Chapter 7 with a generic co-simulation framework for coupling continuous-time and discrete-event simulators. Such co-simulation framework is required by the previously mentioned models and verification methodology.

3

Model Based Design of Embedded Systems

This chapter gives a background on model based design approaches for embedded systems. The focus is on system level design methodologies for digital systems, analog and mixed-signal systems and physical systems. These systems are initially separated since they describe different aspects of a design. In Chapter 4 they are brought together for describing heterogeneous embedded systems.

3.1 System level design

The fundamental principles for modeling digital systems were described by *Gajski* [47] with the diagram shown in Figure 3.1 called the Y-Chart. The axis of the Y-Chart corresponds to three different design concerns and their respective abstractions are represented by four concentric circles. According to the Y-Chart, any embedded system, no matter its complexity, can be described using three types of models. These are behavioral models (also called functional models), structural models (also called net lists or block diagrams) and physical models (also called layout or board design). In addition, models can be described in four main abstractions, represented as concentric circles around the axis origin. The names of the abstraction layers correspond to the type of components generated on each level: transistors on the circuit level, flip-flops and logic

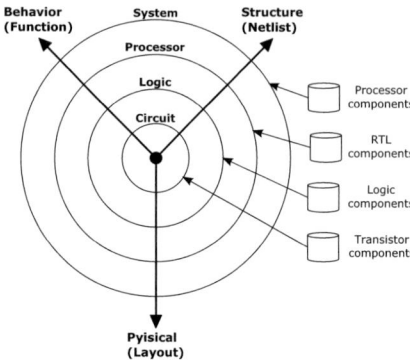

Figure 3.1: Y-Chart [47]

gates on the logic level, ALUs (Arithmetic and Logic Unit) and hardware multipliers on the processor level, and processors, memories and buses on the system level.

3.1.1 Overview

System level design approaches describe embedded systems with models corresponding to the highest abstraction level depicted in the Y-Chart. The separation of design concerns, represented by the three axis of the Y-Chart, makes it possible to independently describe behavioral, structural and physical aspects of a design. The advantages of system level design with respect to lower abstraction design levels such as RTL (Register Transfer Level) are faster simulation speed and increased model reuse. The tradeoff is a lower accuracy due to the high abstraction in which models are described.

System level design methodologies are intended to cope with the increasing complexity of embedded systems and to enhance the productivity of their designers [80]. They are model based design approaches used for the design, refinement and verification of embedded systems. The goals of system level design methodologies can be summarized as follows:

- Enable HW/SW co-design and design space exploration

- Provide effective means for design and reuse

- Facilitate the refinement of models into implementation solutions such as software binaries or RTL models

3.1.2 Design methodologies

The basic components of a system level design methodology are presented in Figure 3.2. An essential part is the orthogonalization of design concerns, i.e., the separation of various aspects of a design to allow more effective exploration of alternate solutions [76]. The most common separations are done between functionality and architecture, and between communication and computation. The different levels of a system level design methodology are described ahead.

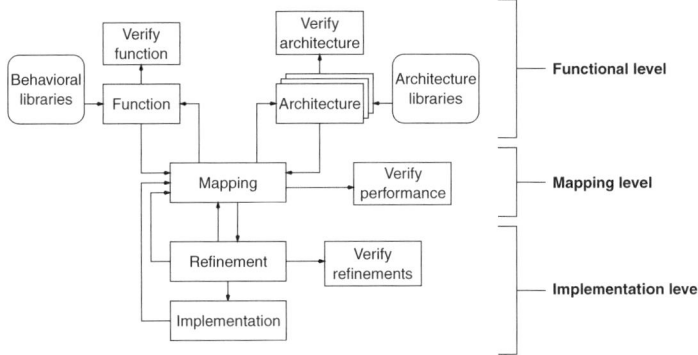

Figure 3.2: System level design methodology for embedded systems [80]

Functional level

The first form of orthogonalization of design concerns is the separation between functionality and architecture. Functionality is described via behavioral models whose execution semantics are described by a particular Models of Computation (MoC). Common MoCs used to describe functional models are Finite State Machine (FSM) or Synchronous Data Flow (SDF) [81] models. They can also be described with imperative MoCs such as sequential programing language like C/C++.

Architectures are system level models of hardware components endowed with I/O ports. Ports are interconnected via signals in order to form net lists. Architectural models are intended to describe the operation of hardware implementation solutions such as software programmable components (DSPs and microcontrollers), fixed hardware components (buses, peripherals and other ASICs) and custom hardware components (FPGAs).

The second form of orthogonalization of design concerns is the separation between communication and computation. This is essential for the reuse of models and for their refinement into lower abstraction models. This is possible by defining the communication semantics between models independent to their performed computations. The separation is done using common design patterns such as interfaces whose implementation is defined by the communication channel they connect to [50]. Communication channel enable the interoperability between models by using things such as adapters, protocols and payloads that define how information is shared.

Mapping level

The process of assigning a function to an architecture is called mapping. For example, a signal processing algorithm corresponding to a functional model can be mapped as a software component in a an architectural model of a microcontroller or it can be mapped as a hardware accelerator in an architectural model of an FPGA.

HW/SW co-design is possible since SW models, corresponding to functional models, and HW models, corresponding to architectural models, can be mapped and tested together. HW/SW co-design can be used to explore the design space in order to optimize a design according to particular metrics and constraints. Such constraints are esti-mated values of performance and costs in terms of resource usage obtained by analytic, simulation or hybrid based methods (refer to Section 3.1.4).

Implementation level

The refinement of system level designs down to the processor level consists of a series of intermediate levels. This process has been described by various authors [25, 34, 42] and vary mainly in the terminology used. Figure 3.3 shows such process according to *Cai and Gajski* [25]. A system level design starts with untimed functional and architectural models mapped into a Specification Model (SM). Following the separation of communication and computation aspects, specification models are refined into approximately-timed models, corresponding to Transaction Level Models (TLM), and finally into Cycle-Accurate Models (CAM). The transformation of computation and communication models does not necessarily need to be done at the same time, which gives rise to models *B*, *D* and *E* from Figure 3.3.

System level design methodologies such as the one shown in Figure 3.2 define how specification models must be described in order to be transformed into Transaction Level Models (TLM) and Cycle-Accurate Models (CAM) models. Each of these models is useful for different design purposes: specification models for conceptual design, TLM models for embedded software programming and CAM models for hardware design. In the end,

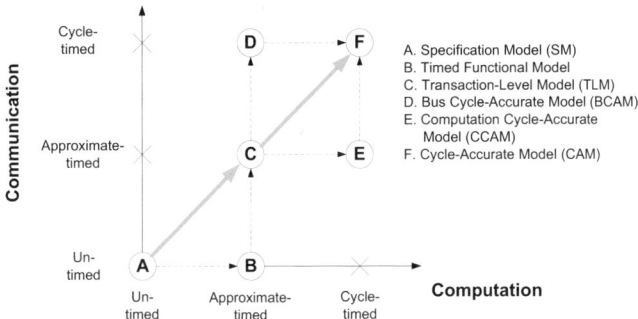

Figure 3.3: Refinement of system level models [25]

regardless of the system level design methodology, the desired implementation result are software binaries ready to be directly loaded into a target processor or synthesizable RTL models for an FPGA target.

Further design methodologies

System level design methodologies had been restricted to the academic domain [10, 28, 36, 61] during the last ten years. Some of the most relevant are the the Metro II framework [36] from Prof. Alberto L. Sangiovanni-Vicentelli and his team at Berkley University and the ESE (Embedded Systems Environment) [28] framework from Prof. Daniel D. Gajski and his team at the University of California Irvine. The Metro II framework is an implementation of Platform Based Design [76] premises and focuses on the automatic mapping of high level behavioral descriptions into architectural models. The ESE framework focuses on the automatic refinement of system level models into RTL descriptions.

The EDA (Electronic Design Automation) market has started to adopted principles from system level design. This has triggered the offering of commercial tools that focus on particular aspects of system level design. Available commercial tools for system level design focus primarily on modeling and simulation using virtual platforms.

3.1.3 System level design languages

Hardware designers for integrated circuits are familiar with models based on the RTL level. The hardware description languages used are VHDL or Verilog. RTL abstractions are adequate for describing hardware and their inherent timing and concurrency, but lack expressiveness to describe embedded software. In contrast, embedded software designers are familiar with programming languages such as C/C++ and assembly languages. These languages are ideal for describing sequential execution of instructions, but lack support for describing timing and concurrency of hardware components.

Languages for system level design describe hardware and software components of embedded system in a high abstraction. They rely on high level programing languages that support modeling concepts from hardware description languages and embedded software programing languages. They support key aspects for describing the behavior and structure of hardware components, such as timing, hierarchy, synchronization and concurrency. They also support embedded software descriptions, which are commonly given as sequential code or using higher models of computation such as state machines or static data flow models.

Some example of system level design languages are SpecC [48], SystemC [55], and SystemVerilog [119]. SpecC and SystemC are based on C and C++ respectively. These are natural languages for describing software components, but not for hardware descriptions. Hardware modeling capabilities are added using extensions (SpecC) or libraries (SystemC). Further details on SystemC are given in Section 3.2. On the other hand, SystemVerilog originates from the Verilog hardware modeling language. SystemVerilog is an extension to Verilog that enables the description of software components.

3.1.4 Verification and validation approaches

In the software engineering community, the terms verification and validation are defined according to the IEEE 1012-2004 standard as follows:

- Verification: "The process of evaluating a system or component to determine whether the products of a given development phase satisfy the conditions imposed at the start of that phase." [72]

- Validation: "The process of evaluating a system or component during or at the end of the development process to determine whether it satisfies specified requirements." [72]

The definitions also apply to system level design with the difference that the end products are models of HW/SW components. Verification is used to check that models are constructed according to their specification (*am I building the model right?*). Validation concentrates on the bigger picture, on whether the constructed model is suitable for the intended application (*am I building the right model?*). Combined, verification and validation provide a certain degree of confidence that a system will behave as expected once it is implemented in a real prototype.

System level design methodologies such as the one showed in Figure 3.2 specify a series of verification steps that may be done in each stage of the design. In each step, a designer needs to make sure that models behave according to their specifications and that they do so in an efficient, safe and deterministic manner. Various verification techniques are available for such purpose and are classified as analytic or dynamic techniques. Analytic techniques rely on formal verification methods and dynamic techniques rely on simulation based methods. This dissertation focuses on simulation based methods for verification purposes. Formal verification methods are not implemented in the work, but they propose an interesting alternative and are thus described ahead.

Formal verification methods

In formal verification methods, the accordance of a model to its specifications is statically checked using a series of mathematical formulations. Instead of requiring a designer to manually check simulation traces for their compliance, formal verification approaches can be automated. They are able to determine all possible states of a model and check for the compliance of specifications accordingly. Unlike simulation approaches, which are limited to checking specifications using a defined set of stimulus, formal approaches are able to check for scenarios which may not have been considered by a designer.

There are three main components to any formal verification method: a *modeling language* in which the system can be described, a *specification language* for the formulation of properties, and a deductive *calculus* or *algorithm* for the verification process [33]. Formal methods rely on mathematical formulations to verify the correctness of a model against formal specifications described in some logical language. They are also able to verify the equivalence between models which have gone through a refinement stage, in which case specifications from an abstract model should be true for a refined model as well. In either case, the process of verification involves the application of the rules of inference of the logic system [9] which provide an absolute answer to a verification problem.

The modeling language must provide a defined set of modeling formalisms, also known as MoCs (Models of Computation). MoCs define available constructs and rules that can be used to describe a system. Typically these MoCs are finite state machines or imperative programing languages. Such rules make it possible to automatically translate models into some sort of abstract mathematical representation which will be used together with formal specifications as an input to the verification process.

Formal specifications use logical languages to describe system properties with precise mathematical notations. Specifications are predicates, meaning that they are evaluated as *true* or *false* by the verification process. Temporal logic descriptions such as linear temporal logic (LTL) and computation tree logic (CTL) are the most widely used type of formal specifications. They enable to express properties such as the occurrence of an event and its properties (event A must occur at least once or infinitely many times), the causal dependency between events (if event A occurs, event B must also occur) and the ordering of events (after every occurrence of event A, event B must follow). They are also able to express many safety and liveness properties of systems. Safety properties are specifications in which "nothing bad happens" during execution. Similarly, liveness properties specify that "something good will happen" during the execution. More details on formal specification languages can be found in [33].

The key difference between formal and dynamic verification approaches is the absence of test patterns. This is possible since the verification process checks for the compliance of specifications over all possible states of a model. The verification process is done using an automatic technique called model checking. Other techniques such as equivalence checking and theorem proving are available and can be found in [49]. Model checking [32] is an algorithmic method for determining whether a system satisfies a formal specification expressed as a temporal logic formula. All reachable states of a model are represented as a Kripke structure, which itself should be a model of the specification formula in order to declare the correctness of a model. The main technical challenge in model checking is the state space explosion problem, addressed by state space reduction techniques. Further details on model checking are out of the scope of this work and can be found in [31–33].

Formal verification methods are adequate for design stages that require some level of automation. This is the reason why they are widely implemented by hardware synthesis back-end tools and by static code analyzers used for software development. Despite their evident benefits, formal verification methods for system level design are not yet widely available in the EDA market, where simulation-based verification is still dominant. Further drawbacks of formal methods are that they limit the expressiveness in which models can be described and, since engineers are not commonly familiar with the mathematical background required to describe formal specifications, these methods are still limited to a small group of design experts.

SPIN [65] and UPAAL [12] are well known model checkers used in both industry and research communities. There are few applications of these in system level design methodologies. Specifically, they are used for checking safety and liveness properties of

SystemC models. In [131], SystemC models were automatically translated into PROMELA language used by SPIN. In [12], SystemC models were automatically translated into timed automata models used by UPAAL. In both cases, safety and liveness properties could be verified. However, the SystemC kernel had to be previously described in PROMELA or timed automata formalisms before SystemC models could be verified. A further application is the Satya framework, which according to their authors [79] can be used for detecting deadlocks, write-conflicts and safety property violation of SystemC models.

Dynamic verification methods

In simulation-based approaches, specifications are checked by executing multiple simulation runs. This process can be done manually or automated via scripts that define test benches and their expected behavior. Specifications are commonly given in terms of behavioral properties that can be verified dynamically during the execution of one or multiple simulation runs. Structural properties do not necessarily need to be verified via simulation. However, since they are mapped together with behavioral specifications, they can also be tested this way.

Simulation is the most widely used method to verify system level models. Models not only describe HW/SW components from an embedded system, but also serve as executable specifications. Their verification is possible thanks to a simulator responsible for the execution of such models and for providing tracing and debugging capabilities.

Simulation-based verification methods vary significantly from formal based methods. Modeling activities in simulation-based approaches do not need to follow strict syntax and semantic guidelines, although they must comply with the basic guidelines dictated by the modeling language. This gives a designer enough liberty to model a system and test it in a simulator in a very short time span. On the other hand, models used by formal methods must follow a strict syntax and semantics in order to be translated into an equivalent mathematical representation which is algorithmically analyzed rather than executed by a simulator.

Simulation-based approaches require test-cases to check for the correctness of a model. In principle, test-cases should have maximum simulation coverage in order to test all possible states of a model. This is commonly done by automating multiple simulation runs. Test-cases are developed using a white box approach, which requires enough knowledge of the model to be tested in order to maximize its simulation coverage. Creating suitable test-cases is a challenging task, even more when the model complexity grows. In such case, it may not be feasible to have complete simulation coverage because developing an ideal test case that can cover all corner-cases is not possible, or because the simulation space is too big. Model-checking techniques also have a similar problem called state space explosion.

The verification of a model and its test cases is done using a simulator that provides mechanisms for tracing and debugging. This verification technique is well known to any hardware or software designer. The only difference is that HW and SW models are verified together. System level simulation provides a new dimension of testing and verification by providing visibility of HW and SW component models at any point of time. This is very useful since HW and SW components work together in order to provide a certain functionality. Debugging capabilities are used to pause or advance simulation time at desired points of time in order to look into a model's state to detect possible bugs in HW or SW. Tracing capabilities are used to record states or values derived from HW or SW components across time. Debugging is typically done manually once a bug is detected and needs to be identified. On the other hand, tracing analysis can be automated up to a certain point using assertions defined in a formal language.

3.2 SystemC

SystemC is the most accepted system level modeling language for system on chip design in the Electronic Design Automation (EDA) community. SystemC was introduced in 1999 by the Open SystemC Initiative (OSCI), which in 2011 merged with the Accellera Systems Initiative [1]. SystemC is an ANSI standard C++ class library [68] that allows modeling and dynamic verification of system level designs in various modeling abstractions. This includes classical RTL hardware modeling up to transaction level design.

SystemC, together with standard C++ software development tools, is used to create system level behavioral and architectural models of embedded systems. They provide hardware and software development teams a virtual platform for design, verification and test purposes without the need of hardware prototypes.

SystemC is both a system level design language and an even-driven simulation kernel. Figure 3.4 shows the layers of the SystemC library. The base layer highlights the fact that SystemC is built on top of C++, which makes it compatible with standard compilers and software development tools. The SystemC standard [68] defines the three middle blocks from Figure 3.4. It defines the simulation kernel and the core language which together provide the main mechanisms for HW/SW co-design. It also defines the data types and elementary channels supporting libraries. The data type library is used for hardware modeling and for certain kinds of software programming, such as bits and bit vector data types for hardware and fixed-point data types for software implementations. Elementary

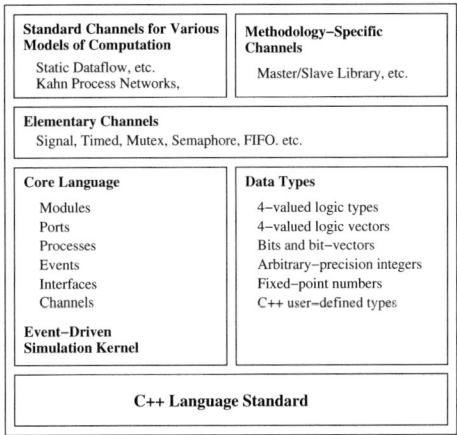

Figure 3.4: SystemC language architecture [55]

channels include basic communication models widely applicable for hardware and software modeling. Finally, the upper blocks are examples of MoCs and methodologies supported by SystemC, but are not included as part of the standard. They provide additional support for specific design methodologies and can be extended or form part of other standards. A condensed summary of the main elements of the SystemC standard is presented ahead. Further information regarding SystemC can be found in [55] and [17].

3.2.1 Structural modeling

The structural components defined by SystemC are modules, ports, interfaces and channels. Figure 3.5 shows an example of a generic SystemC design where such components can be identified. Modules and channels enable the separation between communication and computation aspects of a design. Each of them can be then described in terms of their behavior and architecture. Computation tasks are described inside processes belonging to modules, while communication tasks are described inside channels. Ports and interfaces are used for the interconnection of modules and channels. The following section describes the role of modules and the principles behind their composition for enabling structural hierarchy in a design. The communication aspects of a SystemC design are then presented and classified.

Modules

Modules are the basic building blocks within SystemC used to partition a complex design into smaller and more manageable pieces. A module contains a set of ports, processes and internal data variables. Ports are used to communicate with other modules or channels. Processes are used to describe the functionality and behavior of a module. Internal data variables are used to store a module's states and also for internal communication between a module's processes.

SystemC allows structural hierarchy through the composition of modules, but does not allow behavioral hierarchy. Structural hierarchy means that a module can contain any number of submodules and this embedding can go into any depth. This helps split complex designs into a number of less complex ones in order to hide internal data representation and processes from other modules. Behavioral hierarchy is not possible in SystemC since all processes are treated at the same level, regardless of the hierarchy of the module they pertain to.

Communication Model

Communication in hardware description languages like VHDL and Verilog is described with hardware signals. In contrast, communication in system level designs is described with function calls. These function calls are implemented by a series of ports, interfaces and channels. Channels provide means of communication between modules and between processes within a module. Channels are composed of read/write functions that describe how communication is performed. These functions are accessed by ports using specific interfaces and are explained ahead.

Interfaces are used to publish communication functions defined inside channels. They are declared as abstract classes inherited by a channel that gives meaning to the functions

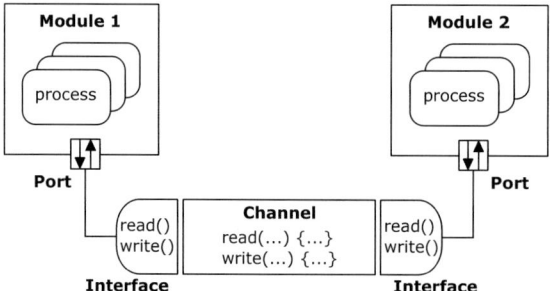

Figure 3.5: Structure of a SystemC design

declared by it. Thus, an interface may have different implementations according to the channel it is associated to. Ports correspond to interfaces, meaning that each port must specify the interface it corresponds to. Consequently, ports have access to the functions declared by their corresponding interfaces; such functions are defined and carried out inside a channel. The basic principle for understanding the communication between ports and channels is as follows: ports are bound to channels through interfaces.

The advance of using ports and interfaces to access a channel is that different versions of a channel can be plugged to the same interface/port combination. Thus, channels can be exchanged or refined according to the stage of the design and modeling needs. This is a common design pattern used in object-oriented designs proven to reduce implementation dependencies: *"program to an interface, not an implementation"* [50].

The SystemC standard includes a series of communication libraries that define basic types of channels and the interfaces and ports to access them. They are called primitive or elementary channels and provide basic means for implementing communication between modules and between processes within a module. Designers are also free to extend primitive channels or create new communication schemes, which is possible thanks to hierarchical channels. More details on both types of channels are given ahead.

Primitive Channels

The most important aspect of primitive channels is that they enable delta-cycle communication delays between concurrent processes thanks to a request-update scheme. This allows deterministic serialization of concurrent activities, e.g. simultaneous read and write requests to a signal. Thus, any operation that may potentially change the state of channels will not have effect until all currently active processes are finished or come to a synchronization point. Primitive channels ensure deterministic communication as long as no implicit communication, such as shared variables, is used to communicate between concurrent processes. Determinism is a desirable property in a design; it ensures that regardless of the order in which concurrent operations occur, the result will always be the same. This is vital for modeling hardware and its inherent concurrency.

Primitive channels provide the following communication mechanisms: hardware signals, buffers, FIFOs, semaphores and mutual-exclusion locks. Hardware signals are similar to VHDL signals, with the exception that SystemC signals support a wider range of signal types. FIFO channels and mutual-exclusion locks rely on the same request-update scheme used by signals and are able to block external calling processes. FIFO channels block calling process on two cases: on write requests to a full FIFO and on read requests to an empty FIFO. Similarly, mutual-exclusion locks block processes waiting for a mutex until it is unlocked and upon which processes are resumed.

Hierarchical Channels

Hierarchical channels differ from primitive channels in the sense that they are able to include other SystemC structures. A hierarchical channel is nothing more than a hierarchical SystemC module implementing multiple internal processes and defining a multiple number of interfaces. They encapsulate structural and communication protocols and are suited for refining primitive channels or to define complex communication structures within a design, such as system-on-chip buses and networks-on-chip.

Hierarchical channels are vital for the interoperability of system level models and for IP reuse. Standardized interfaces and communication schemes, such as the ones defined by the TLM-2.0 communication standard, are implemented with hierarchical channels. This is further described in Section 3.2.4.

Instantiation and Binding

SystemC shares the concept of elaboration with VHDL and Verilog, i.e. all module instantiation and port binding must be completed during the elaboration phase. In terms of object-oriented concepts, instantiation is related to the creation of objects and binding is related to the assignment of function pointers. This applies also for hierarchical modules and channels that may itself require to instantiate and bind structural elements declared inside their constructor.

The execution of a SystemC application consists of an elaboration phase followed by a simulation phase. In the elaboration phase, internal data structures within the SystemC kernel are created. This is done on runtime, during the instantiation and binding of structural components. In this process, each new instance and binding relation is registered to the SystemC kernel. The evaluation phase results in the creation of the module hierarchy.

3.2.2 Behavioral modeling

SystemC models are executed by its simulation kernel based on a discrete-event model of computation (MoC). In a discrete-event MoC, simulation time advances in variable time steps. Time steps are determined on run-time according to timed events stored inside an event queue. The event queue contains a set of timed events that correspond to future points in the simulation time. The event queue changes constantly during simulation since processes are allowed to add or remove events from it. From a behavioral point of view, a SystemC model can be regarded as a network of conceptually concurrent processes that communicate through channels and synchronize on events. In the following, the main concepts behind processes, events and the discrete-event simulation kernel are described.

Processes

Processes are the basic unit of functionality of modules and hierarchical channels. They are used to describe computation or communication functionality in the form of sequential C++ instructions. The SystemC kernel is responsible for the execution of processes. They are executed upon the simulation startup and throughout the simulation according to events declared in their sensitivity list, similarly to HDL languages. SystemC provides two kinds of processes: method processes and thread processes. They are declared using the macros `SC_METHOD` and `SC_THREAD` respectively.

Whenever an *method process* is triggered, it executes until it finishes. It can be invoked any number of times and, most importantly, it cannot be suspended or resumed via *wait()* function calls. Methods do not keep an internal execution state and cannot be used to describe the passing of time.

In contrast, whenever a *thread process* is triggered, it executes until it finishes or until it yields to other processes via a *wait()* function call. Threads keep their internal execution state and can be resumed at the point where they were suspended. The difference between method and thread processes in SystemC is the following: a thread can only be started once and suspended an arbitrary number of times, while a method can be started any number of times, but cannot be suspended.

Events

An event is an object owned by a process or channel used to represent a condition that may occur during the course of simulation and to control the triggering of processes accordingly. These conditions are typically changes of state in a process or of a channel, which cause an event notification. Whenever an event is notified, it triggers the execution of all processes that are sensitive to the event. In addition, the event notification also specifies when sensitive processes are to be executed: immediately, after a delta-delay or after a defined time. An *immediate notification*, invoked by *e.notify()*, causes sensitive processes to be triggered instantly in the current delta cycle. A *delta-delay notification*, invoked by *e.notify(SC_ZERO_TIME)*, causes sensitive processes to be triggered at the same time instant, but after updating primitive channels, i.e., in the next delta-cycle. Finally a *non-zero notification*, invoked by *e.notify(t)* where $t > 0$, causes sensitive processes to be triggered after a designated amount of time.

Processes may be sensitive to events either statically or dynamically. Static sensitivity is allowed for method and thread processes, while dynamic sensitivity is only allowed for thread processes. Static sensitivity is used to define the events which a process is sensitive to. It must be declared before the simulation begins and corresponds to the static sensitivity list of processes. Dynamic sensitivity can only be declared by thread processes and this is done during simulation. Dynamic sensitivity overrides the sensitivity list of a thread. Threads use dynamic sensitivity as a mechanism to yield their execution to other processes, thus suspending themselves, and to designate a specific event it wishes to wait on, after which the thread resumes its execution. Dynamic sensitivity is invoked via *wait()* function calls implemented in any of its variants.

3.2.3 Simulation semantics

The scheduler is the part of the SystemC kernel. It is responsible for timing and execution control of processes, even notification handling and for updating communication channels. The scheduler follows the elaboration phase, once all structural components are instantiated, bounded and the structural hierarchy is complete. Like VHDL and Verilog, the SystemC scheduler is based on a discrete-event MoC and on the notion of delta-cycles.

In a discrete-event MoC, simulation time advances in variable steps according to events stored in an event queue [138]. They correspond to SystemC `sc_event` objects, owned by processes or channels and handled by the SystemC kernel. Events in the queue are organized in a time-stamp order representing future points in time in which events will be notified in order to trigger sensitive processes. The event queue contains the necessary information to determine how simulation time will advance in future points of time. However, the event queue may continuously change due to executing processes either adding more events to the queue, or rescheduling or canceling existing ones.

The notion of delta-cycles is used for the simulation of conceptually concurrent processes, which must be treated as sequential processes running on a computer. Delta-cycles do not increase simulation time, and an arbitrary finite number of them may be executed at any point in simulation time. They are used to implement delta-delay notifications and to enable the request-update scheme of primitive channels.

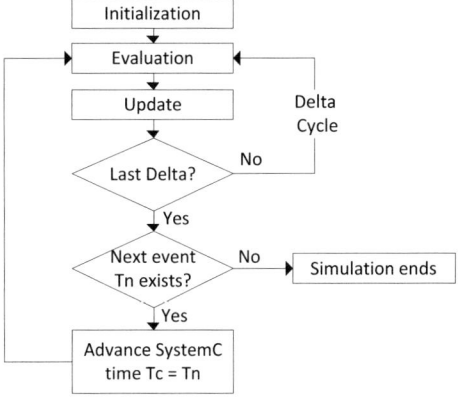

Figure 3.6: SystemC scheduler

The SystemC scheduler is non-preemptive. This means that when processes are executed, they may not be interrupted by any other process until they finish (SC_METHOD) or they yield via a *wait()* function call (SC_THREAD). A designer must be aware of SystemC's non-preemptive scheduler in order to avoid simulation deadlocks. Thread processes are particularly interesting in this case, since they yield control back to the scheduler either by waiting for an event or by waiting for a given period of time to elapse. Deadlocks happen when such process blocks the execution of other processes by either not yielding or by waiting for an event that is never notified. Further information regarding deadlock identification in SystemC models by formal means is available in [63, 131].

The behavior of the SystemC scheduler is presented in Figure 3.6. Its simulation semantics are described informally in its IEEE standard [68] and are summarized as follows:

1. *Initialization.-* During the initialization phase, every process is executed once, unless the contrary is specified. The order in which processes are executed is unspecified, however deterministic in all simulation runs using the same simulator version.

2. *Evaluation.* All runnable processes are executed in an arbitrary order. If there are immediate notifications, the corresponding processes become part of the runnable processes and are executed in the same delta-cycle.

3. *Update.* Primitive channels that requested an update in the evaluation phase are updated.

4. *Delta-cycle.* Notify all the delta-delay notifications generated during the evaluation and update phase. This may result in a new set of runnable processes, in which case steps 2 and 3 are repeated.

5. *Timed events.* Timed event notifications are considered when there are no more runnable processes, no update requests and no delta-delay notifications. Simulation time T_c is advanced to the time of the next event T_n, and all the time events due to occur at that specific time are notified. Steps 2 - 4 are repeated. Whenever time is advanced, the scheduler also checks to see if the simulation time has reached the optional stop time specified as an argument to *sc_start()*.

6. Simulation is finished when there are no runnable processes, update requests, delta or timed event notifications. Simulation is also aborted if *sc_stop()* is called, or if a run-time error occurs.

3.2.4 TLM-2.0

The role of Transaction Level Models (TLM) in the refinement of system level models was introduced by *Cai and Gajski* [25]. The term TLM is used to describe system level models annotated with estimated values of communication and communication times. Computations are grouped in blocks of sequential instructions annotated with execution times. Communication aspects in transaction level models are implemented via software calls between processes and may include timing annotations. This in contrast to RTL abstraction models, where communication is implemented with signals that require multiple events at the level of individual bits and bytes. For example, a TLM model would represent a read or write request to a bus as a single function call, while an RTL model would require such request to be described on a pin- and cycle-accurate manner using a series of signal assignments and signal read operation occurring on the wires of a bus. Thus, the simulation performance of TLM modes is magnitudes of time faster than RTL models.

Transaction level models have been used in various forms for many years [120]. The language in which they are typically described is SystemC, which enables the creation of virtual prototypes for use cases such as embedded software development, architectural exploration and functional verification. The reason why TLM models have been widely described in SystemC is due to the emergence of the modeling standards TLM-2.0 (forms part of the IEEE 1666 standard [70] since 2011) and IP-XACT [71] (describes an XML scheme for TLM-2.0 models).

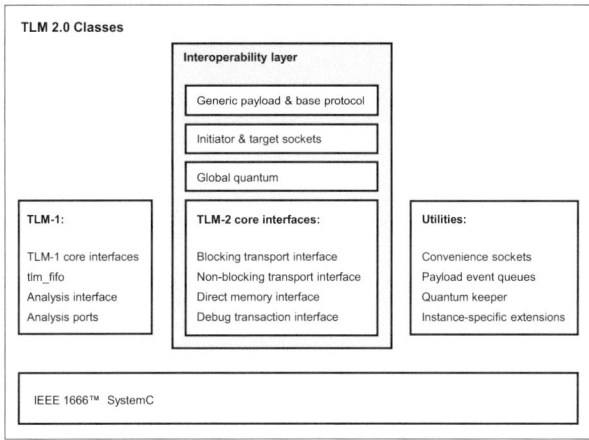

Figure 3.7: TLM-2.0 language architecture [70]

The TLM-2.0 standard defines a set of classes layered on top of the SystemC class library as shown in Figure 3.7. The TLM-1 set of classes are included to provide compatibility with older models, but are completely separate and incompatible with newer classes from the TLM-2.0 version. The TLM-1 standard defines a set of core interfaces for transporting transactions by values or constant references, which are not suitable for describing memory mapped buses. Instead, the interoperability layer from the TLM-2.0 standard provides a set of classes for modeling memory mapped buses and other on-chip communication networks. It is composed of core interfaces, sockets, generic payload, and base protocol meant to be used together in concert. The third set of classes are utilities, provided for convenience and to help ensure a consistent coding style. The utilities do not belong to the interoperability layer and are not a requirement for interoperability.

Coding Styles

TLM-2.0 defines two coding styles: loosely-timed and approximately-timed. Coding styles are conventions used to describe temporal aspects of the communication in a memory mapped bus.

The *loosely-timed (LT)* coding style makes use of the blocking transport interface. This interface assigns two timing points to communication transactions, marking the start and the end of a transaction. These two timing points may occur at the same simulation time, in which case the transaction is untimed, or at different times. The loosely-timed coding style is appropriate for the use case of software development using a virtual platform model. Virtual platforms may include instruction set simulators, timers, interrupts

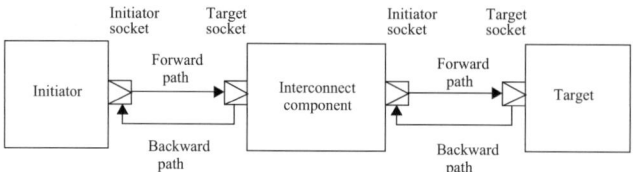

Figure 3.8: TLM-2.0 connectivity [70]

and peripheral models, and are capable of booting a complete operating system. The loosely-timed coding style may implement temporal decoupling, which means that each process keeps track of its local time and is allowed to run ahead the simulation time until it reaches a synchronization point, also called *global quantum.* Temporal decoupling permits a significant simulation speed improvement by reducing the number of context switches.

The *approximately-timed (AT)* coding style makes use of the non-blocking transport interface and is appropriate for architectural exploration and performance analysis use cases. In the approximately-timed coding style, transactions are assigned multiple timing points apart from the start and end of the transaction. Processes need to run in lock-steps with the SystemC simulation time, which decreases simulation speed in relation to the LT coding style, but increases the amount of detail and timing accuracy involved in a transaction. The approximate-timed coding style is suitable for describing communication protocols that require multiple phases and timing points during the lifetime of a transaction.

Connectivity

Figure 3.8 shows how the connectivity between initiators, interconnect and target modules is implemented. Initiators are able to start a transaction, i.e. creating new transaction objects and pass them on by calling a method of the transport interface (blocking or non-blocking). A target is a module that acts as the final destination for a transaction. An interconnect component is a module that forwards transactions from initiators to targets.

Forward and backward paths are used to call methods of a transport interface in both directions. They are implemented via initiator and target sockets which must be bounded. An initiator socket provides a port and export for the forward and backward paths respectively. Similarly, but only in the opposite direction, a target socket provides a port and export for the backward and forward paths respectively.

Core interfaces

The TLM-2.0 core interfaces define standardized methods to pass information between initiators and targets. They play a key role in module and IP-reuse, since modules sharing the same type of core interfaces, regardless of the details of their implementation, should be compatible and able to communicate with each other. The core interfaces consist of the blocking and non-blocking transport interfaces, the direct memory interface (DMI) and the debug transport interface.

The *blocking transport interface* is used to support the loosely-timed coding style. The blocking transport interface is appropriate for an initiator that completes a transaction with a target during the course of a single function call. The only timing points of interest are those that mark the start and the end of the transaction.

The *non-blocking transport interface* is used to support the approximately timed coding style. It is appropriate for modeling the detailed sequence of interactions between initiator and target during the course of each transaction. Transaction are broken down into multiple phases, each one associated with a timing point.

The *Direct Memory Interface (DMI)* and *Debug transport interface* are specialized interfaces that provide direct access and debug access to an area of memory owned by a target. DMI is intended to accelerate regular memory transactions in a loosely-timed simulation, whereas the debug transport interface is for debug access free of the delays or side-effects associated with regular transactions.

3.3 Virtual prototypes

Virtual prototypes are system level simulation models that emulate (mimic) the behavior of hardware prototypes. A useful definition provided by Synopsys is the following:

> "Virtual prototypes are fast, fully functional software models of systems under development executing unmodified production code and providing a higher debugging/analysis efficiency." [124]

Virtual prototypes are composed of system level models of processing elements and peripherals, such as memories, buses, interrupt controllers, etc. In particular, processing elements are models of software programmable components, such as traditional micro-controllers and DSPs, and hardware programmable components, such as customized FPGA processing elements. The abstraction in which these models are described is typically on the TLM level, where communication and computation components are already identified and provide approximate-timing information (refer to Figure 3.3). Altogether they enable the full simulation of a complete embedded system on a host computer.

Virtual platforms can be used in most stages of a design. For instance, in early design stages, virtual platforms are used as executable specification models that capture HW and SW requirements in a high abstraction. Due to their high abstraction, they can be made available in very little time and can serve as golden reference models for further development and refinement stages. Virtual platforms can also be useful after the deployment of a product. For instance, they may be used by a software designer to verify software updates, in the form of firmware or higher level functionalities, done on multiple versions of deployed products which may not be physically available at the moment of testing the update. They can also be provided to customers for effects of training and technical support.

The main applications of virtual prototypes are during the development phase. They are especially useful in the following cases: software-driven verification and software development. Software-driven verification is equivalent to software-in-the-loop testing, where production code can be verified inside a virtual platform along with a simulated environment. This facilitates the verification process without the need of real hardware prototypes and experimental setups. Virtual platforms are also very useful for software development. Initial software applications and drivers can be developed and tested using virtual platforms. This allows the identification of software bugs and communication bottlenecks, which might be too complicated to find in real prototypes. Aside from the previously stated verification benefits, virtual prototypes enable many other testing capabilities such as SW performance optimization, SW centric power analysis and fault injection.

3.3.1 Processor models

Processor models are system level descriptions of processing elements, such as DSPs and microcontrollers, used in embedded systems. They are responsible for the simulation of binary code compiled for particular processor architectures and for their communication with other components inside a virtual platform.

As any other system level model, processor models are composed of structural and behavioral descriptions. Structural descriptions contain architectural details of a processor such as functional units, pipelines, caches, registers, counters, I/Os, etc. Behavioral descriptions correspond to a software application that is loaded into the system model.

Timing information is afterwards obtained by the combined interaction of structural and behavioral descriptions. The questions are: how are structural and behavioral descriptions done and what type of timing information can they provide?

There are two main approaches to the previous questions: analytical and simulation approaches. Analytical approaches obtain timing information of a processor model by performing a formal analysis of pessimistic corner cases on the system level model [116]. This analysis provides worst-case/best-case execution times (WCET/BCET) of all functions in a software application. Such information is vital in systems with hard real-time constraints, e.g. an ABS application in the automotive domain. An example of a state-of-the-art commercial solution providing such type of analysis is aiT from AbsInt [4]. The second approach to the timing estimation is via simulation. As mentioned earlier in Section 3.1.4, simulation cannot ensure the complete coverage of corner cases, but it is adequate for verifying the functionality of a virtual prototype and for obtaining approximate timing information from it, something which is not possible by analytical approaches. Since the focus of this dissertation is on dynamic verification, only simulation based approaches are presented ahead.

The behavior and timing information of a processor model is dictated by an Instruction Set Simulator (ISS). An ISS is used to perform binary translation of a software application complied for a specific microprocessor or DSP instruction set and to execute it in a host computer. Instruction set simulators are classified into two main categories according to how the binary translation process is done: interpreters and binary code translators, also called the just-in-time (JIT) compilation [102].

Interpretive ISS

Interpretive ISS mimic the fetching, decoding and execution phases performed by processors. The binary translation process consists of fetching, decoding and executing one binary instruction at a time in a loop-wise fashion until all instructions are executed. This process is done completely on run-time, similarly to how it is done in hardware. This straightforward mapping of hardware behavior to a software simulator has a major disadvantage: low simulation performance. In particular, the instruction decoding is a time consuming process in a software simulation [111]. On the other hand, the advantage of interpretative ISS is that they provide the highest degree of simulation accuracy, i.e. cycle-accuracy. SimpleScalar [118] and ArchC [112] are two well-known interpretive ISS in the academic domain. In the commercial domain, the ISS provided by popular embedded software IDEs (e.g. IAR Embedded Workbench [67], Code Composer Studio [126], μVision [8]) are typically interpretative since they provide very detailed information about the behavior of a processor with cycle-accuracy and do not require high simulation efficiency.

Binary code translators (emulators)

The second type of ISS relies on a binary code translation technique called just-in-time (JIT) compilation. JIT compilers perform translation of target instructions into native instructions on run-time, just before instructions are executed. Native instructions correspond to instructions compatible with the host architecture, typically an x86 or x64 PC. Target instructions are grouped into basic blocks that, after being translated into their native equivalent, are stored in a cache. This improves simulation performance, making sure that translation does not occur for subsequent executions of the same basic block [18]. ISS relying on JIT compliers are better known as *emulators*, since the instruction set of a target architecture is emulated by the architecture of a host machine. The benefit of emulators is a very high simulation performance in relation to interpretative ISS. However, the translation process does not take into consideration any micro-architectural details regarding pipelines and caches, and thus cannot provide cycle-accurate timing information. Instead, emulators are considered instruction-accurate simulators since they are able to emulate the execution of target code on an instruction basis. Timing information is obtained with the assumption that each instruction from the target's instruction set is executed in a fixed number of cycles, a factor called Instructions Per-Cycle (IPC).

The most relevant open-source emulator is QEMU [13], which supports a wide range of target architectures used by embedded systems. Another open-source example developed by academia is SimSoc [62] from INRIA. Emulators are also the de-facto technology for processor models in state-of-the-art virtual prototyping commercial solutions like CoMET-METeor from Synopsys Virtual Prototyping [121], Simics from Wind River [45] and OVP Processor Models from Imperas [73] (also used by Cadence Virtual System Platforms [24]). A study regarding the available models and simulation performance offered by some of these tools can be found in [88].

Integration into SystemC

Emulators result very attractive for SystemC based virtual prototypes due to their high simulation performance. In order to form part of a virtual prototype, processor models are wrapped inside SystemC modules provided with TLM-2.0 communication interfaces. Wrappers make it possible for the SystemC scheduler to control the execution of an emulator and its communication with other components of the virtual prototype. Further information on how SystemC wrappers are created for processor models and their underlying ISS can be found in [14, 15, 110].

3.3.2 Open Virtual Platforms (OVP)

Open Virtual Platforms (OVP) [73] is a commercial emulation tool that provides component libraries with a wide variety of executable models of processors and peripherals used for constructing virtual prototypes. OVP solutions are useful for embedded software development and software-in-the-loop tests of any type of embedded systems, especially for SoC and MPSoC applications.

Models are executed by a proprietary simulator called *OVPsim*. OVPsim is a state-of-the-art commercial simulator for virtual prototypes which offers various debugging and analysis capabilities for verification purposes. Some of these capabilities are: instruction and task level debugging and profiling, memory footprint analysis and semi-hosting of a target's I/O functionalities in a host computer. OVPsim includes a simulator for peripherals, accessible via an interface called Peripheral Modeling Interface (PPM), and a simulator for processor models, accessible via an interface called Virtual Machine Interface (VMI). The simulator used for processor models is based on the just-in-time (JIT) compilation technique described in Section 3.3.1. Thus, all processor models from OVP provide instruction-accurate timing information.

All executable models available by OVP are provided with code wrappers that make them compatible with the SystemC and TLM-2.0 standards. In addition, OVPsim is provided with APIs in order to be controlled by an external simulator for co-simulation purposes, namely a SystemC kernel acting as simulation master. Therefore, OVP virtual prototypes are completely interoperable in a SystemC simulation environment, such as the application shown in Figure 3.9. The application shows two OVP models: an ARM Cortex-M3 processor model and a UART peripheral model. These models are wrapped in SystemC and communication via TLM-2.0 interfaces with native SystemC peripheral models such as a memory mapped bus, memories, ADC, interrupt controller and a GPIO used for activating an LED. The execution of the virtual prototype is carried out by the SystemC kernel, which is responsible for the co-simulation with OVPSim. This co-simulation scheme is seamlessly integrated into SystemC and adds a very small simulation overhead.

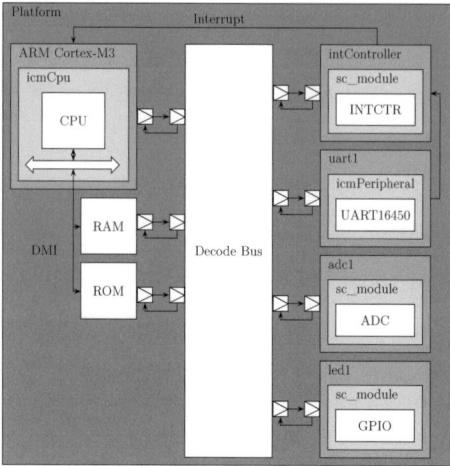

Figure 3.9: Integration of OVP in a SystemC virtual prototype [113]

3.4 Analog and Mixed-Signal (AMS) modeling

Section 3.1 through Section 3.3 presented methodologies, verification approaches and
languages for the design of digital components of embedded systems. Up to this point,
embedded systems have been considered as digital systems, made up of digital HW
components and SW applications. Such assumption is intentionally done in order for
system level models to be compatible with discrete-event simulators such a SystemC.
Such systems are commonly used to perform computation-intensive tasks that transform
digital information by means of complex digital signal processing techniques, e.g. data
compression, signal coding and video image detection. However, embedded systems are
also reactive systems used to interact with their environment via sensors and actuators.
This is illustrated in Figure 3.10. They require more than just digital models in order
to be described. This has given rise to multi-domain modeling approaches that include
physical and analog mixed-signal (AMS) models.

3.4.1 Physical domain modeling

Physical systems are described based on a continuous time (CT) model of computation.
Such descriptions are done using mathematical models composed of sets of simultaneous
equations with boundary values and initial conditions. In particular, these mathematical
models are differential and algebraic equations (DAE). DAE descriptions must abide to
the physics of the system that is being described, such as Kirchhoff laws for current

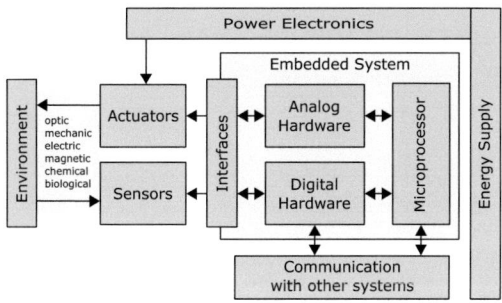

Figure 3.10: Structure of an embedded system [125]

and voltage in electric circuits or dynamic equilibrium laws in mechanical and thermo-dynamic systems. Therefore, the CT model of computation is adequate for describing systems from multiple physical domains such as electrical, electromagnetic, mechanical, optical, thermal, etc.

The behavior of a system of DAE equations is obtained when solved by either analytical or numerical techniques. Analytical techniques are suitable for solving systems of equations by hand, but may not be feasible for complex systems of equations. Instead, numerical techniques are commonly used since they can be implemented by a computer algorithm called numerical solver or numerical simulator. A numerical simulator is able to solve a set of DAE equations at each point of simulation time in order to obtain its behavior. Numerical solvers are an essential part of any CT simulator. They can be classified according to the type of equations they are able to solve: implicit differential-algebraic equations (DAE) or explicit ordinary differential equations (ODE).

Noncausal models

DAE are by essence written in an implicit form, meaning that both unknown and known variables can appear on both sides of the equation. The standard form of a DAE is as follows:

$$f(\frac{\vec{dx}}{dt}, \vec{x}, \vec{y}, t) = 0 \tag{3.1}$$

where $\vec{x}$ is a vector of differential variables (the derivatives with respect to time appear in the equation, also referred to as state variables), $\vec{y}$ is a vector of algebraic variables and t is an independent scalar variable.

Physical models described via DAE equations in implicit form are *noncausal models*. A typical characteristic of noncausal models is that their behavior is not described in terms of input/output. Prominent examples of noncausal modeling and simulation tools are: Modelica [97], VHDL-AMS [69], the Simscape [128] extension from Simulink and MapleSim [86].

The advantages of noncausal modeling according to [52] can be summarized as:

- Noncausal modeling is the most natural form to describe physical systems of equations

- Noncausal models are more declarative for describing systems on a high abstraction, focusing on *what* to model rather than *how* to model

- Noncausal models are more reusable than causal models

Causal models

The description of physical models commonly starts with noncausal models. However, the use of state-of-the-art modeling and simulation frameworks for noncausal models is still limited to a small group of academia and industry experts. In practice, noncausal models (Figure 3.11a) are manually translated into causal models (Figure 3.11b) using symbolic manipulation.

Causal models are described with Ordinary Differential Equations (ODE). An ODE is a relation that contains functions of only one independent variable, and one or more of their derivatives with respect to that variable. They are written in explicit form such that unknown variables appear on the left hand side of the equation and known variables on the right hand side of the equation. The standard form of an ODE is as follows:

$$\frac{d\vec{x}}{dt} = f(\vec{x}, t) \tag{3.2}$$

where $\vec{x}$ is a vector of differential variables and t is an independent scalar variable.

Causal modeling remains the most commonly used paradigm since multiple numerical integration methods are available for solving ODE equations, as well as commercial tools that can implement them. Causal models are described in terms of inputs/outputs and thus can be implemented by actor-oriented simulation frameworks that support a continuous-time model of computation. Prominent examples of causal modeling and simulation tools are: the MATLAB ODE Suite [117] used by Simulink and LabVIEW. In addition, these tools are de-facto in the industrial automation domain.

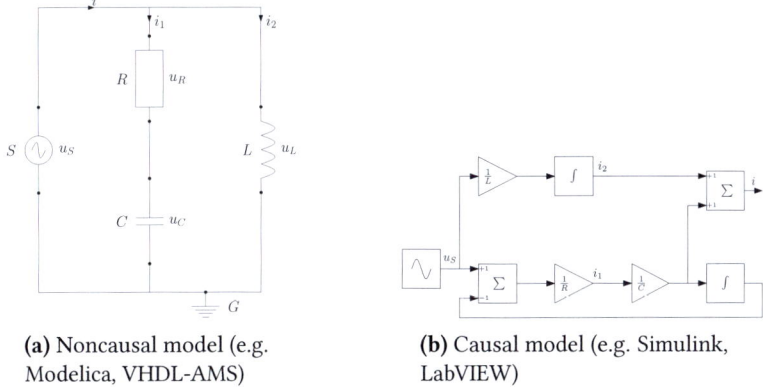

(a) Noncausal model (e.g. Modelica, VHDL-AMS)

(b) Causal model (e.g. Simulink, LabVIEW)

Figure 3.11: Equivalent noncausal and causal representations of an RCL circuit [52]

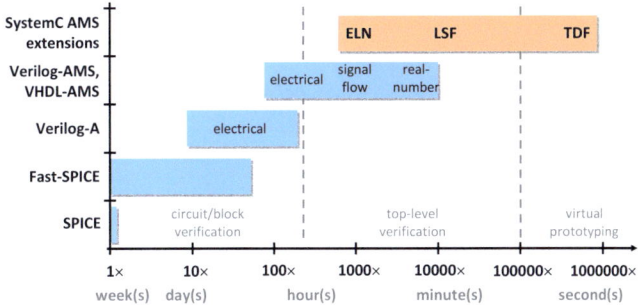

Figure 3.12: Simulation performance comparison of analog and mixed-signal simulators[11]

3.4.2 Analog and mixed-signal modeling languages

Languages like VHDL-AMS and SystemC-AMS provide an improved simulation efficiency with respect to SPICE based simulations as shown in Figure 3.12. This is due to the abstraction in which physical systems are described, typically as ODE equations, which is sufficient for performing verification in a virtual prototype environment. Models described in such languages are executed by coupled digital and analog simulators. A description of both languages is presented ahead.

VHDL-AMS

The VHDL-AMS modeling language is defined by the IEEE 1076.1 [69] standard as an extension of the VHDL language standard IEEE 1076-2002. It provides modeling and simulation capabilities for causal and noncausal analog and mixed-signal (AMS) systems.

VHDL-AMS models are compatible with standard VHDL digital models. The coupling between digital and AMS models is implemented by a VHDL-AMS simulation engine.

The VHDL-AMS language supports many abstraction levels in electrical and non-electrical energy domains. It supports three types of dynamic verification techniques: transient analysis, frequency domain small-signal analysis and noise simulation analysis. Further details on VHDL-AMS modeling guidelines and verification capabilities can be found in [9].

VHDL-AMS is considered a multi-domain language since it is able to describe the behavior of physical energy domains such as electrical, magnetic, translational, rotational, fluidic, thermal and radiant. The key concept behind this is the identification of physical effort and flow variables necessary for describing behavior in each domain. Effort and flow concepts are called *across* and *through* quantities respectively. Some examples of across and through quantities are: voltage and current in the electrical domain, velocity and force in the mechanical translation domain, angular velocity and torque in the mechanical rotational domain, pressure and volumetric flow rate in the fluidic domain, among others. Quantities together with the physical laws for each domain are used for describing sets of DAE equations in VHDL-AMS.

The VHDL-AMS standard defines how analog solvers for systems of DAE equations, namely numerical simulators, should interact with a discrete-event simulator for VHDL digital designs. The numerical and discrete-event simulators are coupled using a co-simulation scheme. This co-simulation scheme forms part of the *simulation cycle* described in the VHDL-AMS standard. Further details on this respect can be found in [30, 69].

Available commercial simulators for VHDL-AMS language are SMASH [40] from Dolphin Integration, SystemVision [93] from Mentor Graphics, Saber [123] from Synopsys and Simplorer [7] from ANSYS.

SystemC-AMS

The SystemC-AMS language is an extension to the SystemC language. It enables analog and mixed-signal modeling and simulation capabilities. SystemC-AMS is not yet defined by an international standard, although a detailed documentation [106] and its respective proof-of-concept simulator [46] are available.

SystemC-AMS extensions are fully compatible with the SystemC language standard as shown in Figure 3.13. The architecture of the SystemC-AMS language follows a layered approach built on top of the SystemC kernel. The *user level layer* corresponds to the two top levels of Figure 3.13 and supports the following MoCs: Electrical Linear

Networks (ELN), Linear Signal Flow (LSF) and Timed Data Flow (TDF). The *solver layer* provides a linear DAE solver for ELN and LSF models and a scheduler for TDF models. The *synchronization layer* is responsible for embedding MoC descriptions and their solvers/schedulers into data flow cluster processes [132] able to co-simulate together with SystemC's discrete-event simulator.

The ELN MoC supports the modeling of noncausal continuous-time models described as electrical networks. Electrical network are built by the instantiation and interconnection of basic passive components derived from available macromodels, such as resistors, capacitors and inductors, as well as sources and monitors. ELN does not support the use of non-linear elements (e.g. transistors and diodes), although there are some workarounds [5, 26]. A further limitation relies on the available linear DAE solver provided in the recent SystemC-AMS proof-of-concept simulator. The solver implements simple fixed-step numerical integration methods (a combination of backward Euler and trapezoid methods [59]) which may lead to numerical instabilities.

The LSF MoC supports modeling of continuous-time systems described in a causal form using the following basic blocks: additions, multiplications, integration and delay. The connection of such blocks is used to define systems of equations, similarly to MATLAB/Simulink, which can be solved by the available linear DAE solver. The same limitations with respect to the linear DAE solver apply as before.

The TDF MoC is an implementation of the Synchronous Data Flow (SDF) [81] principle, where processes are statically scheduled according to production and consumption rates. The advantage of TDF is the possibility to describe applications using a MoC similar to SDF. This is very useful for modeling digital signal processing algorithms. A further benefit is high simulation efficiency, since the TDF static scheduler reduces the dynamic overhead imposed by the discrete-event kernel of SystemC.

SystemC-AMS is not yet a fully capable multi-domain simulator. It provides basic modeling capabilities for AMS systems in the electrical domain, but it lacks the modeling support for describing other type of physical energy domains. In addition, the available linear DAE solver in proof-of-concept simulator [46] is not robust enough, although improvements on this sense have been investigated [59].

3.4.3 Verification and validation approaches

The definition of the terms verification and validation in the context of physical modeling differs from those used in the software engineering community (refer to the definitions given in Section 3.1.4). A useful definition done by American Institute of Aeronautics and Astronautics is as follows:

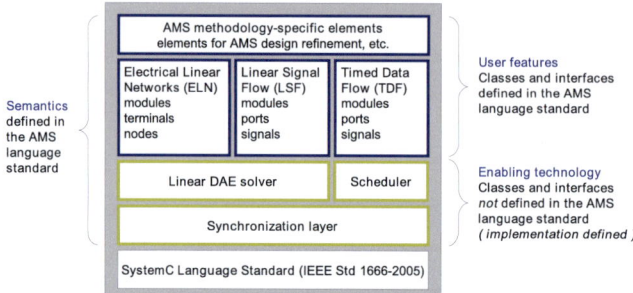

Figure 3.13: Architecture of the SystemC-AMS language [105]

- Verification: "The process of determining that a model implementation accurately represents the developer's conceptual description of the model and the solution to the model." [6]

- Validation: "The process of determining the degree to which a model is an accurate representation of the real world from the perspective of the intended uses of the model." [6]

The verification and validation of physical models relies on numerical simulation and statistical analysis techniques. The process of verification and validation is crucial for qualifying and building credibility on the correctness and accuracy of models for specific scenarios. A high level view on verification and validation processes for physical models is presented in Figure 3.14. The diagram, referred to as the Sargent Circle [115], presents the role of modeling and simulation (black solid lines) and assessment activities (red dashed lines) in the verification and validation process.

In Figure 3.14, the *reality of interest* represents the physical system whose behavior needs to be obtained. A *mathematical model* based on physical laws is created for describing the behavior of the physical system. The mathematical model is a set of algebraic and differential equations with boundary values and initial conditions. A *computer model* is then created based on causal and noncausal forms of the mathematical model. The computer code must be verified against the mathematical model in order to check that it is correctly implemented and that the solver provides the desired results. A computer model is then validated against the reality of interest in order to quantify the accuracy and correctness of a model.

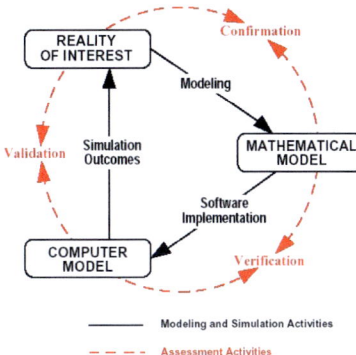

Figure 3.14: Verification and validation of physical models [115]

Verification process

As stated above, verification is the process of checking the correctness of a computer model with respect to a mathematical model. According to [127], the verification process can be divided into a series of steps called: code verification, calculation verification and uncertainty quantification. *Code verification* checks for possible errors that may result during the translation of mathematical models into forms compatible by a numerical simulator. *Calculation verification* checks for numerical errors introduced by the numerical simulation. It involves adapting parameters of the solver such as the simulation time step and error convergence tolerances. *Uncertainty quantification* uses model predictions based on probabilistic analysis. Model predictions are used to perform sensitivity analysis tests and to quantify the effects of random and systematic errors.

A considerable amount of time must be spent in analyzing the impact of uncertainties. The reason for this is that model predictions, which are based on probabilistic analysis, may generate enormous amounts of information when simulated. Probabilistic analysis remains the most widely used and accepted uncertainty analysis method. Alternate methods for uncertainty quantification are available such as symbolic-simulation. Further details regarding uncertainty analysis and the comparison between available methods can be found in [54, 64].

Validation process

Verification deals with the mathematics associated with the model, whereas validation deals with the physics associated with the model. A common statement used for the validation of physical models is as follows: *get the physics right!*. In other words, if the physics used to describe a model are correct, then so must be the model that describes it. In order to check this premise, the validation process must quantify the accuracy of a model with respect to experimental data and determine its confidence interval.

A key principle in the validation process is delimiting the amount of metrics before starting the validation process. A validation metric is the basis for comparing features from experiential data with model predictions [127]. These model predictions are available from the verification phase. Experimental setups must be adapted for obtaining specific validation metrics, which influence the way in which they are constructed. In any case, if the validation process does not comply with the requirements, a model and its experimental setup must be revised.

4

Heterogeneous Embedded Systems

Industrial devices are considered throughout this dissertation as heterogeneous embedded systems. The term heterogeneous results from a system level perspective and it refers to the combination of digital systems, analog and mixed-signal systems and multi-domain physical systems. This implies the use and coupling of different models of computation that can describe the different continuous and discrete dynamics of such systems.

This chapter describes available models of computation for describing behavioral aspects of heterogeneous embedded systems. It presents state-of-the-art work that have overcome the challenge of coupling models of computation for performing verification and validation of heterogeneous embedded systems. Finally, the state-of-the-art is evaluated regarding requirement for the design of industrial devices in order to define the scope of this dissertation.

4.1 Models of computation

According to [138], a model is defined as an abstract representation of a system, entity, phenomenon or process. In order for models to be interpreted by everyone without ambiguity, they are described using physical, mathematical or logical representations with clearly defined syntax and semantics. Such representations are known as modeling formalism or Models of Computation (MoC) [83]. The purpose of a model of computation is to support the specification of a system's descriptions and to facilitate its verification. From a designer's point of view, MoCs are the means a designer has to his disposal for describing and verifying a system.

A model of computation refers to a language or class of languages with a common syntax and semantics. MoCs are equivalent to modeling paradigms, each being more or less suited for describing different parts of a system. According to [83], a MoC determines three sets of rules for a model: *(1)* what constitutes a model, *(2)* its concurrency mechanisms, and *(3)* its communication mechanisms.

4.2 Combining models of computation

Various MoCs are typically required to describe different parts of an embedded system and its environment. They are heterogeneous systems since the composition of multiple MoCs determine the behavior of a system. Some examples of commonly used MoCs are: Synchronous Data Flow (SDF) [81] for digital signal processing algorithms, Finite State Machines (FSM) and sequential programing languages for software components, Discrete-Event (DE) for digital hardware components and Continuous-Time (CT) for physical systems.

The combination of Discrete-Event (DE) and Continuous-Time (CT) models of computation are called hybrid system[23]. Hybrid systems are used to describe reactive systems [57] made up of digital models with discrete dynamics and plant models with continuous dynamics.

Cyber-Physical Systems (CPS) are also hybrid systems. According to [75, 82], in CPS systems the computations and communication tasks carried out by a digital system are influenced by the behavior of the physical processes they interact with and vice-versa. The overall behavior of a CPS system does not only depend on a digital system being able to perform a certain task, but on the conjoined interaction between digital and physical systems. From a model-based perspective, CPS systems can be described as hybrid systems, therefore they are equivalent. The only difference is that the term CPS has been popularized during the last years.

Models that follow a particular MoC can be executed together by a simulator that understands the syntax and semantics of the MoC. In this context, a model can be seen as a set of rules, equations, or constraints for generating I/O behavior [138]. Thus, a simulator is an agent capable of obeying the instructions in a model, as well as its concurrency and communication mechanisms, in order to obtain its behavior.

Simulating the behavior of hybrid systems requires continuous-time (CT) simulators for their continuous dynamics and discrete-event (DE) simulators for their discrete dynamics. The simulators involved must be coupled to obtain the composite behavior of a hybrid system. This presents an additional challenge since the MoCs behind CT and DE simulators are very different from each other. Two main approaches are identified for coupling DE and CT models of computation: formal based approaches and co-simulation based approaches.

4.2.1 Formal-based approaches

Formal approaches to heterogeneity define the semantics for the interoperation between heterogeneous MoCs according to a set of formalized descriptions. Formal approaches to heterogeneity require a holistic simulation framework that understands the details of the MoCs being coupled and that can implement the interoperation semantics accordingly.

In these types of approaches, the coupling semantics as well as the MoCs involved must have a formal mathematical representation. MoCs are formalized according to three orthogonal aspects: how they implement sequential behavior, the available communication mechanism and the available concurrency mechanisms. The formalized interoperation semantics describe the control and communication aspects required for the interoperation of heterogeneous MoC. Creating such formalized descriptions requires considerable effort and full access to the simulation kernels involved. Their advantage is that their implementation can be automated, thereby leaving no room for misinterpretations.

Ptolemy II

Ptolemy II [44] from the University of California Berkeley is an actor-oriented simulation framework used to study the complexity derived from the heterogeneous combinations of MoCs. Ptolemy II has implementations of many models of computation including Synchronous Data Flow, Kahn Process Networks, Discrete Event, Continuous Time, Synchronous/Reactive and Modal Models.

The Ptolemy II project started in 1996 and has been in active development ever since. A key aspect of Ptolemy II is that each MoC and its interoperation semantics have a formal mathematical background. The interoperation semantics are initially abstract and are defined according to the MoCs being coupled. Their implementation is done

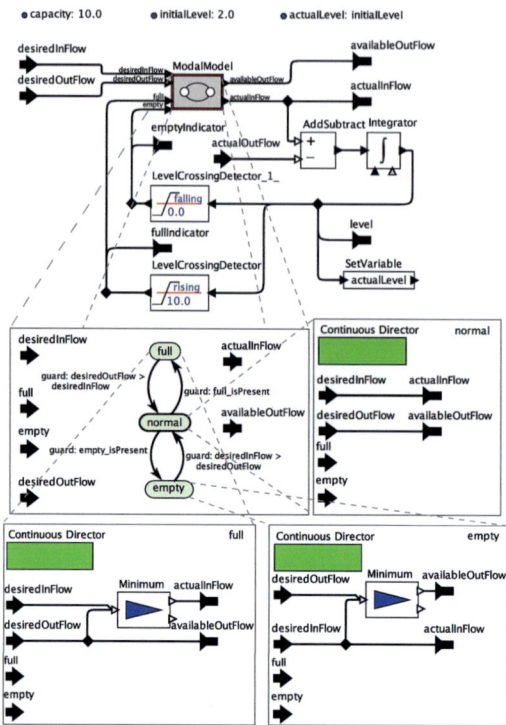

Figure 4.1: Ptolemy II: Model of a fuel tank using modal models [38]

in a Java-based framework that includes a graphical front-end for building models using drag-and-drop component libraries and a simulator as back-end. Due to its ample modeling and simulation capabilities, Ptolemy II is being used as basis for the commercial simulators MLDesigner [96] and VisualSim [94].

Ptolemy II supports the coupling of DE/CT MoCs in hybrid systems with modal models. Modal models [84] are hierarchical FSM descriptions that encapsulate the behavior of other MoCs. The transition between FSM states are controlled by a DE director and each state of the FSM is controlled by a CT director. CT directors rely on ODE solvers (fixed- and variable-step solvers) for simulating the behavior of physical systems. Figure 4.1 shows an example of modal models in Ptolemy II for modeling the behavior of a fuel tank and its controller. In this example, one modal model describes three different operation modes (labeled as *full, normal, empty*) of a fuel tank based on their internal state, each of them is respectively controlled by a CT director.

DEV&DESS

DEV&DESS is a modeling formalism developed by Prof. Bernard P. Zeigler, a pioneer in modern modeling and simulation theory. DEV&DESS [138] stands for Discrete Event and Differential Equation System Specification. It is an extension of the DEVS formalism from the same author that enables DE and CT modeling and simulation. It includes both DEVS (Discrete Event System Specification) and DESS (Differential Equation System Specification) formalisms; each of them is respectively equivalent to DE and CT MoCs.

DEV&DESS provides a mathematical background that describes the composition semantics of DEVS and DESS modeling formalism. However, there are currently no simulation framework that implement the DEV&DESS formalism. Instead, its DEVS counterpart has attracted more interest in industry and academia, and for which various simulation frameworks are available, such as CD++ [135] and DEVS/HLA [85].

Further references

According to [87], heterogeneous system level design is a relatively new area of research. Its goal is to provide support for the design of complex digital systems such as SoCs and MPSoCs. Some of the best-known frameworks in this area are: ForSyDe [114], SystemC-H [108], Metro II [36] and SML-Sys [87]. All of these frameworks provide support for the modeling and composition of heterogeneous MoCs. However, none of these provide modeling formalisms for describing physical systems.

4.2.2 Co-simulation based approaches

Co-simulation is a common approach for addressing the integration of different MoCs and their simulators. It is based on the coupling between simulation engines, each of them focusing on a specific part of a model, in order to obtain the behavior of a full system. Co-simulation is a useful approach for the dynamic verification of systems whose behavior cannot be otherwise obtained by a single simulation engine.

The simulation of hybrid systems requires two types of simulation engines: discrete-event (DE) simulators for discrete dynamics and continuous-time (CT) simulators for continuous dynamics. The first one enables the verification of HW/SW descriptions; the later allows the verification of physical systems described via sets of differential and algebraic equations. An entity, which might be one of the simulation engines or an external computer program, must implement a clearly defined co-simulation algorithm. The co-simulation algorithm defines the interoperation semantics for the control and communication between simulation engines.

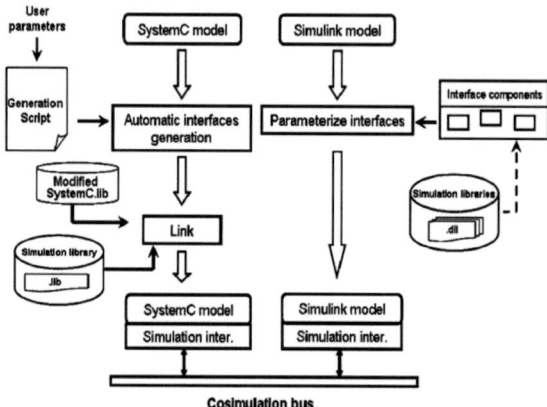

Figure 4.2: CODIS tool flow [21]

SystemC is used throughout this dissertation as the main discrete-event modeling and simulation framework. Therefore, related work on co-simulation approaches for coupling SystemC with continuous-time simulation tools are initially presented. Afterwards, further approaches using tools other than SystemC are presented.

SystemC and Simulink

The CODIS (<u>Co</u>ntinuous/<u>Di</u>screte <u>S</u>imulation) [21] framework is an academic co-simulation tool for coupling continuous and discrete simulation models from Simulink and SystemC. It describes a tool flow for generating control and communication interfaces for Simulink and SystemC models and a co-simulation algorithm for coupling their execution. An overview of this tool flow is illustrated in Figure 4.2. In this approach, SystemC digital signals and Simulink analog signals must connect to input/output interfaces in order to share information. These interfaces communicate to a co-simulation bus responsible for transferring data between models running on different simulators. The co-simulation bus is also responsible for transferring control commands emitted by SystemC, which acts as simulation master, and Simulink, acting as simulation slave. Most importantly, the co-simulation algorithm is efficient since the simulation time is decoupled, i.e. simulators do not need to run in fixed simulation steps as done in [20, 60]. Thus, the major contribution of CODIS is the implementation of an efficient co-simulation algorithm between SystemC and Simulink.

Synopsis Platform Architect [122] is a virtual prototyping tool for SystemC models. It offers a co-simulation interface for SystemC and Simulink models. The co-simulation algorithm performs synchronization on fixed steps. Therefore, an adequate synchronization step size must be manually chosen to meet the simulation speed and accuracy requirements.

SystemC and electric circuit simulators

The work by *Kirchener et. al.* [77, 78] describes the co-simulation of SystemC and the electric circuit simulators SwitcherCad and Saber. The co-simulation algorithm is similar to the one used by CODIS and is embedded into a SystemC module, which makes SystemC the simulation master. In order to ease usability, the interconnection of signals is done via a signal pool where all sinks and sources coming from SystemC digital signals and SwitcherCad/Saber analog signals are connected to.

Ptolemy II and continuous-time simulators

Ptolemy II already provides DE/CT modeling and simulation capabilities. In addition, Ptolemy's CT directors have already enough capabilities to solve complex physical models thanks to a set of available ODE solvers (fixed- and variable-step). However, there are applications in which external CT simulators may be preferred for a number of reasons. This is the case for Building Controls Virtual Test Bed (BCVTB) [136], a software environment based on Ptolemy II and its co-simulation with the CT simulators: Energy-Plus, Simulink, Dymola (Modelica). In BCVTB, Ptolemy II acts as simulation master which all other CT simulators connect to thanks to dedicated communication and control interfaces.

BCVTB is used to model building heat transfer, HVAC (heating, ventilation, and air conditioning) system dynamics and control algorithms. Although the application field does not directly apply to the design of embedded systems, from a research perspective, it is interesting to see the extent to which co-simulation can be applied. From a technical point of view, the implemented co-simulation algorithms are simple since they perform synchronization on fixed simulation steps. According to its author, more efficient algorithms relying on adaptive synchronization time steps are not implemented in BCVTB due to technical limitations from the CT simulators.

Functional Mock-up Interface

The Functional Mock-up Interface (FMI) [98] was initially developed by Daimler AG with the goal to improve the exchange of simulation models between suppliers and OEMs as illustrated in Figure 4.3. The latest version of the FMI (ver. 2.0) was published in 2012 as a result of the European project MODELISAR.

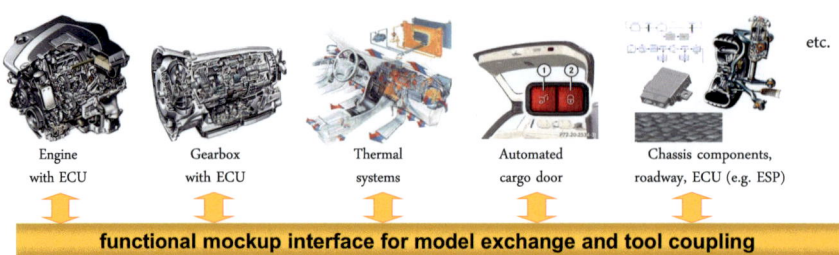

| Engine | Gearbox | Thermal | Automated | Chassis components, |
| with ECU | with ECU | systems | cargo door | roadway, ECU (e.g. ESP) |

functional mockup interface for model exchange and tool coupling

Figure 4.3: Applications of the Functional Mock-up Interface (FMI) [98]

The FMI standard defines guidelines for (1) the exchange of dynamic models between tools, and (2) for the coupling of simulation tools in a co-simulation environment. In the first case, FMI for model exchange is intended for tools that can generate C-code from dynamic system models made of differential, algebraic and discrete-time equations, and for tools that can import and evaluate them. In other words, the FMI exchange interface standard defines as common wrapper for dynamic system models originating from different modeling environments and described in C-code. These models and their wrappers can be transferred to any other simulation environment and evaluated using a single simulation engine.

In the second case, the FMI for co-simulation is intended to provide a common interface standard for coupling two or more simulation engines. The synchronization between simulation engines are restricted to discrete communication points based on fixed or variable time-steps. The interfaces provide standard C-based functions for sharing information between one simulator acting as co-simulation master and one or more simulators acting as co-simulation slaves. However, the FMI for co-simulation interface does not specify the semantics for sharing information between master and slave simulators. This is also known as the co-simulation algorithm and used to control and synchronize the flow of information between different simulators. On the other hand, the advantage of the FMI co-simulation interface is that it provides enough means for implementing simple or complex co-simulation algorithms.

Further references

The dissertation from *Marcel Verhoef* [134] emphasizes the importance of multi-domain models for the early verification of embedded control systems. He defines embedded control systems as computing systems that are intimately coupled to the environment which they monitor and control. This definition is equivalent to *Lee*'s [82] definition of cyber-physical systems.

Verhoef provides a pragmatic solution for multi-domain modeling and simulation intended for two different types of engineers: control engineers and software engineers. His solution is based on the co-simulation of DE and CT system level descriptions. The simulators used for this purpose were VDM++ for DE and 20-SIM for CT. VDM++ is a general purpose model oriented formal specification language that enables round-trip engineering with UML. VDM++ also provides a simulation engine based on a DE MoC which makes it possible to verify software architecture specifications on early design stages. On the other hand, 20-SIM is a commercial CT modeling and simulation tool for dynamic systems. 20-SIM relies on a graphical framework for building models using Bond graphs, state space descriptions, block diagrams and equations. It provides enough expressiveness for describing most type of physical energy domains, similarly to VHDL-AMS and Modelica. *Verhoef* defines communication and control interfaces for transferring information and commands between both simulators. The implementation of the co-simulation algorithm is carried out in VDM++ which is used as the simulation master.

4.3 Scope and definition of this work

The scope of this dissertation is on model based design approaches of embedded systems for industrial devices. The design challenges encountered during their design and the open issues that will be accordingly addressed in this dissertation were presented in Section 2.4. The most relevant issues include finding appropriate model-based approaches for describing structural and behavioral aspects of embedded systems and approaches for verifying such descriptions together with physical models of plants and environments. Further issues include supporting different stages of the development life-cycle, i.e. from the point a measurement or control principle is identified up to its implementation in a prototype and experimental setup. In between these stages, appropriate model-based design approaches must be found for helping embedded software developers, hardware developers and physicists to communicate and test design specifications in a better way.

Chapter 3 described the state-of-the-art on model-based design approaches for embedded systems. The distinction was initially done between approaches for modeling digital systems and approaches for modeling analog and mixed-signal systems. In the first case, the SystemC framework and virtual prototyping technologies were introduced. In the second case, analog and mixed-signal frameworks such SystemC-AMS and VHDL-AMS were presented.

Chapter 4 showed that embedded systems for industrial devices do not exclusively fall in one of these two categories. Instead, they are a combination of both, where the behavior of digital hardware and software components are intertwined with the behavior of analog and mixed signal components and physical processes. Hybrid systems provide an adequate model-based approach for describing such systems. They are the result of combining modeling approaches for digital and physical domains. The state-of-the-art on model-based design approaches for hybrid systems was described in the previous section. These originate from a purely academic background, such as Ptolemy II and the DEVS&DESS formalism, and from industry-orient applications, such as the FMI interface and diverse co-simulation approaches using tools like SystemC, Simulink, and analog circuit simulators.

The focus of Ptolemy II [44] framework is on creating a strong mathematical background for the composition of different models of computation. The available modeling formalisms and their high level of abstraction make Ptolemy II a valuable tool in early design stage. However, Ptolemy II cannot be used in a system level design methodology since it does not contemplate the refinement of communication and computation aspects of actors (actors in this sense are defined as software components that execute concurrently and communicate through messages sent via interconnected ports). Formal based modeling approaches such as the DEV&DESS [138] formalism suffer from similar limitations. Their strict modeling guidelines render the refinement of models a very challenging task.

Commercial actor-oriented frameworks such as MATLAB/Simulink and LabVIEW also do not consider the refinement of communication and computation aspects of actors. Instead, these tools focus on the design and verification of behavioral models in early design stages. Moreover, these tools are capable of automatically converting models into hardware or software descriptions. During this conversion process, there are no intermediate steps for performing architectural exploration of a design or for adding architectural details regarding computation or communication aspects of a design. Such capabilities are only considered by system level design methodologies via a series of subsequent refinement steps.

Refinement is an intrinsic part of system level languages like SystemC [68]. Its transaction level modeling (TLM) standard supports this and provides interfaces for communication models described in different abstractions. SystemC is the most adequate language for system level design of digital hardware and software components of embedded systems. Moreover, it is widely supported by different tool manufactures and IP vendors.

The analog and mixed-signal modeling limitations of SystemC are addressed by an AMS extension. However, SystemC-AMS [106] has still many limitations with respect to its modeling capabilities of physical systems and with respect to the solvers it supports for their evaluation. In comparison, VHDL-AMS [69] has improved modeling capabilities for physical systems and supports the use of more efficient solvers. However, digital modeling capabilities of VHDL-AMS are intended for RTL abstractions, which is not adequate for system level design methodologies.

The FMI [98] for co-simulation interface is intended to provide common interfaces for coupling two or more simulation engines. It defines APIs that tool vendors must implement in order to couple their simulators in a co-simulation environment. However, the FMI interface does not define the implementation of co-simulation algorithms, also called master algorithms. Co-simulation algorithms are necessary to control the data exchange between subsystems and the synchronization of simulation engines.

Bouchhima et. al. [21] , *Kirchener et. al.* [78] and *Verhoef* [134] describe the implementation of discrete-event/continuous-time (DE/CT) co-simulation algorithms for the following simulation engines: SystemC & Simulink, SystemC & Saber, and 20-SIM & VDM++. Further examples of the implementation of simpler DE/CT co-simulation algorithms are presented in the work of *Wetter* [136] and *Borland et. al.* [20] for the simulators: Ptolemy II & Energy-Plus/Simulink/Dymola and SystemC & Simulink.

The authors mentioned above implement DE/CT co-simulation for the design and verification of different applications of hybrid systems, e.g. industrial systems, automotive systems and HVAC systems. However, none of these authors consider the use of co-simulation during multiple stages of the development life-cycle of embedded systems. In all these cases, co-simulation is used to verify models in a common abstraction. The refinement of such models and the new dimension of verification capabilities that they enable have not been investigated. Moreover, none of the above-mentioned approaches considers the use of advanced virtualization tools together with DE/CT co-simulation for the creation of multi-domain virtual prototypes.

The focus of this dissertation is on the creation of a problem-oriented verification strategy for heterogeneous embedded systems based on system level design methodologies. It is applicable throughout initial design stages and up to the implementation of a system in hardware prototypes and experimental setups. The type of heterogeneous systems considered are hybrid systems described with continuous and discrete dynamics.

This goal of the problem-oriented verification methodology proposed in this work is to provide multidisciplinary team members enhanced verification capabilities to identify and solve design problems during early development stages. This is possible by coupling the execution of different simulators, each one responsible for obtaining the behavior of part of a system. The combined execution of simulators can help increase the understanding of interdependencies between different system components. This eventually helps increase the confidence in the correctness of a design, thereby reducing risks in a project and leading to hardware prototypes and experimental setups that are built right the first time.

5

Guidelines for the Construction of Virtual Prototypes

This chapter describes initial considerations from the industrial automation domain with respect to the creation of virtual prototypes of industrial devices. It also describes an integrated design flow for heterogeneous embedded systems that supports the use of virtual prototypes. Finally, a set of guidelines are given for the construction of consistent and meaningful virtual prototypes. These guidelines are intended to ease the creation of virtual prototypes and to increases the reusability of designs.

5.1 Initial considerations

5.1.1 Modeling requirements

The acceptance of any new design methodology in an organization is determined by its compatibility and support for ongoing best-practices. Non-technical aspects should also be considered, such as the level of acceptance among design experts and the overhead that this might bring.

A series of interviews with design experts in the industrial automation domain permitted to gather initial requirements regarding the types of models needed for the creation of virtual prototypes of industrial devices. At the moment of the interviews, none of the consulted design experts had previous experience with related virtual prototyping approaches. The design experts consulted where mainly embedded software engineers, hardware designers with expertise in digital and analog design, and physicists with experience on complex measurement principles. The following requirements where extracted from such interviews:

- *Hardware models.* Industrial devices typically rely on off-the-shelf hardware components such as peripherals, microcontrollers and DSPs to implement functionality. Only in particular cases, FPGA implementations with commercial and proprietary IP-cores are required. Therefore, the hardware models as well as the description language used must be adequate for both types of applications. In addition, the hardware models used must be equivalent in terms of computation and communication capabilities as those used in ongoing or previous projects.

- *Software models.* Embedded software contains a vast know-how of a company's software engineering practices. This know-how must be captured by a software model instead of developing new models that can mimic it. Therefore, available legacy code, real-time operating systems and proprietary component-based software frameworks must be imported by software models in order to be reused.

- *Physical models.* Physicists and control engineers tend to describe physical processes using domain-specific modeling and simulation tools. In order to reuse available physical models, the domain-specific tools in which they are developed must be made compatible with the aforementioned hardware and software models.

- *Tooling*: New tool must be compatible with existing tool flows. Tooling acceptance not only relies on technical compatibility issues, but also on their adherence to current practices. Therefore, new tools must also provide certain level of familiarity and acceptance with embedded system designers.

5.1.2 Modeling domains

According to [138], a model is defined as a physical, mathematical, or logical representation of a system, entity, phenomenon or process. The representation of a model is done via a set of modeling formalisms, that have a mathematical foundation, support formal or semi-formal reasoning and have a definite semantics. From an engineer's point of view, formalisms are the means at his disposal in order to describe a system.

Industrial devices are classified as hybrid systems [23] since their behavior is described by continuous and discrete dynamics. In the first case, continuous dynamics are used to describe models from the physical domain. In the latter case, discrete dynamics are used to describe models form the digital domain. Therefore formalism for physical and digital domains must be considered for the creation of virtual prototypes.

Physical domain models

Continuous dynamics are inherent to physical systems whose behavior is naturally described by continuous time-dependent functions. Continuous dynamics are used to describe the behavior of physical systems from different domains, e.g. electrical, mechanical, optical, thermal, etc. The process variables are continuous such as temperature, pressure and flow in the case of process automation systems, or voltage and current in the case of power automation systems.

Models of the physical domain are described using sets of simultaneous differential and algebraic equations that are piecewise continuous functions of time. They are a natural system specification formalism used in domains such as electrical, mechanical, optical, thermal, etc. Their simulators are classified according to the modeling form they support: *causal* or *non-causal*. *Causal* models are formulated in terms of explicit equations, for example, ordinary differential equations (ODE). Examples of simulators for causal models are Simulink and LabVIEW. *Non-causal* models are formulated in terms of implicit equations, for example, differential algebraic equations (DAE). Examples of simulators for non-causal models are Modelica and VHDL-AMS.

Digital domain models

Discrete dynamics are used to describe the behavior of hardware and software component of embedded systems. For instance, they can be used to describe the behavior of hardware blocks such adders and multipliers in different abstractions. They can also be used to describe the behavior of software component using sequential programming languages or other higher-order models such as statecharts and finite state machines.

Models of the digital domain operate on a discrete time basis with outputs that are piecewise constant function of time. *Untimed* MoC such as synchronous reactive modes and data flow models use simulators where models are evaluated on fixed intervals. Early versions of Ptolemy II and Matlab Stateflow are examples of simulators for digital untimed models. *Timed* MoC such as timed data flow models, discrete event system specifications (DEVS), Register Transfer Level (RTL) models and Transaction Level Models (TLM) use event based discrete simulators where time advances in variable periods called events. Simulators for digital timed models are commonly used for hardware description languages such as VHDL and SystemC.

5.2 Role of virtual prototypes in the design flow

Figure 5.1 shows an extension to the traditional design flow of embedded systems described in Section 2.3. The extension is marked in gray and corresponds to a system level modeling stage. The proposed design flow is called Integrated Design Flow since it enables an integrated design and verification of system level models of hardware, software, mixed-signal and analog components. This is possible thanks to the addition of system level modeling stage after the algorithmic modeling stage. During the system modeling stage virtual prototypes are constructed in various granularities for exploring the design space and for performing HW/SW co-design once a system has been partitioned.

This integrated design flow takes into consideration current practices in the design of embedded systems for industrial devices. As a result, tradition design approaches are not affected by the proposed design flow. Instead, they are extended with further design and verification capabilities. Each design stage from Figure 5.1 is described ahead.

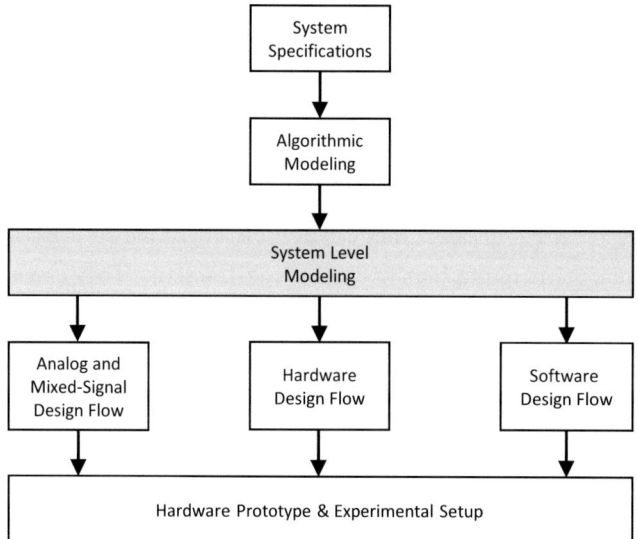

Figure 5.1: Integrated design flow for embedded systems

5.2.1 System specifications

System specifications are based on functional and non-functional requirements. Functional requirements describe the particular measurement or control principles that need to be implemented in an embedded system, as well as boundary conditions for its operation. Non-functional requirements include things like operation temperature range, safety considerations, robustness considerations, the desired power consumption, footprint and cost, etc. Specifications are commonly given in textual form and as mathematical equations. Other approaches include using UML-diagrams, but this is almost exclusively done for software descriptions.

5.2.2 Algorithmic modeling

Behavioral descriptions of an embedded system and its environment are modeled in this stage according to the system's specifications. Descriptions rely on high-level modeling paradigms such as data flow models and statecharts. Commonly used software tools in this stage are the actor-oriented frameworks MATLAB/Simulink and LabVIEW. Both tools provide enough modeling capabilities for describing the behavior of embedded systems using discrete-time models and physical systems using continuous-time models.

Digital models are composed of discrete-time actors such as statecharts and discrete signal flow blocks. These models are used to describe the behavior of an embedded system. At this point, the distinction between HW and SW has not yet been done, which provides enough modeling expressiveness. This decision is done in the system level design stage, where adequate means for describing HW and SW implementations are available.

Physical models are composed of continuous-time actors such as continuous data flow blocks, transfer functions and state space representations. These models are used to describe physical systems and are useful to simulate environments that are equivalent in terms of their behavior to experimental setups. Simulink and LabVIEW provide an adequate modeling and simulation framework for such purpose. In addition, both tools support model-in-the-loop testing, where discrete-time and continuous-time models are able to interact with each other as shown in the example of Figure 5.2. Other domain-specific tools may be used at this stage. Such tools provide further specialized means for describing physical systems, e.g. Bond Graphs, Modelica, AMS models.

The verification process of a digital model may be done using rapid prototypes or via model-in-the-loop testing. Rapid prototypes are capable of executing behavioral models in real-time and are able to interact with real experiential setups. Rapid prototypes may

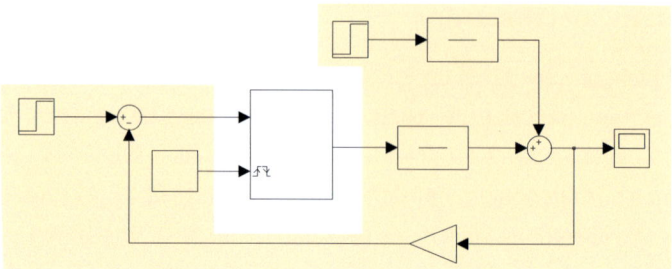

Figure 5.2: Example of an algorithmic model of a close-loop control application

be dedicated pieces of hardware or standard PCs communicating via a set of specialized interfaces. The second and most common type of verification is via simulation means, which may be simpler than using rapid prototypes and experimental setups. This type of verification is called model-in-the-loop testing and requires physical models that can reproduce the behavior of a well-known physical system.

Example

The example shown in Figure 5.2 shows a typical application for algorithmic modeling using Simulink. Discrete-time models are marked in blue and continuous-time models in yellow. This example shows a very basic feedback control application where a PID algorithm, which will be later on implemented in an embedded system, is tested together with environment models. The behavior of the PID algorithm is implemented using an available PID block from Simulink's discrete time toolbox, while the environment is modeled using standard transfer functions and signal flow blocks. This type of testing is called model-in-the-loop testing and is a common practice in the industry. In this particular case, model-in-the-loop testing will help obtain adequate proportional, integral and derivative constants for a PID controller. Its main advantage is a very low modeling effort, which makes it possible to test multiple controller and plant models in a very short time span.

5.2.3 System level modeling

The transition from algorithmic modeling to system level modeling requires further considerations. It assumes that the algorithmic modeling stage provides two types of models: physical models that describe the behavior of an environment and digital models that describe the behavior of an embedded system. These models will be further used as follows:

- Physical models are provided with special I/O interfaces to communicate with digital models. Apart from that, they are not modified and will be further utilized in the system level design stage together with their native simulator.

- Digital models must be translated into sequential C/C++ code. The translation can be done manually or using available code generation tools (e.g Simulink Coder [130]). The obtained code must be purely functional and hardware independent. Special I/O interfaces are provided later on for the communication with physical models.

C/C++ code descriptions are purely behavioral and implementation-agnostic, i.e. they do not contain any detail in terms of how they implement their behavior. A design decision must be made in order to assign a behavioral model to an architectural model. In system level design, this decision is called mapping (refer to Figure 3.2) and results in a design's HW/SW partitioning. A behavioral model may be mapped to a SW implementation if the architectural model corresponds to a software programmable processing element, e.g. a microcontroller or DSP. The second possibility is to map a behavioral model to a HW implementation if the architectural model corresponds to a hardware element, e.g. off-the-shelf components such peripherals, memories, buses or hardware accelerators in FPGAs. Further details with regards to system level design and mapping activities were mentioned in Section 3.1.1.

The introduction of system level modeling in a design flow enables two useful design and verification mechanisms: HW/SW co-design and software-in-the-loop testing. HW/SW co-design is intended to aid embedded software engineers and is possible thanks to the adoption of SystemC as modeling language and simulation kernel. A methodology for the design and verification of such SystemC models will be described in Section 6. Software-in-the-loop testing is intended to aid control engineers and is possible thanks to specialized interfaces and a generic co-simulation algorithm between SystemC and virtually any domain-specific continuous-time simulator for AMS (analog and mixed-signal) models. The mechanism used to co-simulate SystemC models with continuous-time simulators are described in Chapter 7.

The result of combining system level models of HW/SW and AMS components are virtual prototypes with multi-domain simulation capabilities. The advantage of a multi-domain system level simulation framework becomes clear when one recalls that embedded systems are used to interface with their physical environment [43]. Often, they are coupled and cannot be tested in separation. Having a framework where physical and digital domains can interact in a correct and reproducible manner opens up new design and verification capabilities for embedded system designers. Further details on this co-simulation framework are described in Chapter 7.

Virtual prototypes are extremely useful for software engineers since they can be used to verify embedded software without the need of a development board or hardware prototype. Virtual prototypes can speed up the software development process since embedded software can be developed and tested before any hardware implementation is available. Even hardware-dependent software [41] development such as firmware, device drivers and RTOS related tasks is possible thanks to available peripheral and processor models. Moreover, the use of virtual platforms has been gaining acceptance in the industry. Further information on this topic can be found in [113], where a detailed evaluation on the use of virtual prototypes in the design of embedded systems for industrial devices was presented.

Virtual prototypes can also be used by control engineers for software-in-the-loop testing in a multi-domain system level simulation framework. Such type of testing not only enables the verification of software, but also the verification of complete embedded systems made of application software, hardware dependent software and hardware models.

Example

Figure 5.3 shows an example of the close-loop control application presented earlier in Section 5.2.2. Since the application was originally developed inside a Simulink framework, Simulink will be further utilized for this example, although any other continuous-time simulation tool can be used for this purpose. Physical system models were not modified, whereas the embedded system model, corresponding to a PID block from Simulink's discrete time toolbox, was transformed into C-code. The resulting C-code, which is simply an imperative representation of a PID algorithm, was imported into a SystemC model and made available to Simulink as a user-defined block (labeled as *Digital Controller* in Figure 5.3).

The block labeled as *Digital Controller* is a virtual platform of an embedded system. It contains system level models of processing elements, buses, peripherals and analog front end models. Digital I/Os and analog interfaces form the virtual platform are able to communicate with Simulink signals.

The embedded system model from Figure 5.3 is a virtual prototype that provides valuable behavioral and performance information about a real embedded system. Its co-simulation together with a physical system is not only useful to verify the behavior of the PID software application, but also to verify hardware dependent software and

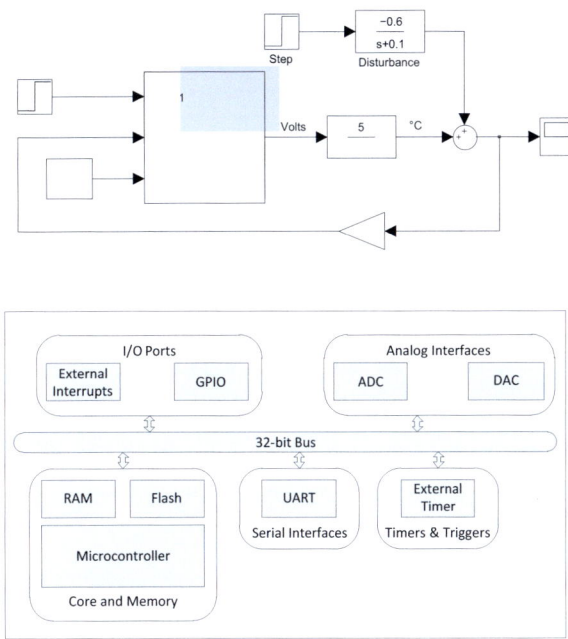

Figure 5.3: Example of a system level model of a close-loop control application

hardware models from the virtual prototype. Therefore, design faults can be identified and corrected in a very short time span, before going further into detailed design stages. This eventually helps increase the confidence of a design, avoiding redesign stages in the implementation phase.

5.2.4 Specialized design flows

The expected outcome of a system level design flow is a clearly defined partition of HW, SW and AMS component models. Components available as off-the-shelf components do not require further development. Those which require further development are handed over to specialized design flows.

Hardware models requiring implementation in an FPGA must be translated into HDL descriptions. The translation of SystemC models to HDL descriptions can be automated with high-level-synthesis tools [35] which are starting to become available to the common public in the EDA market (e.g. the Vivado Design Suite [137]). SystemC models can also be translated manually into HDL descriptions which requires a considerable design effort. HDL descriptions are then handed over to specialized hardware design flows.

IDEs for hardware design are provided by major FPGA vendors, e.g. Xilinx, Altera, Actel, Lattice Semiconductor and Atmel. The expected outcome is a bit file for a specific FPGA target.

Analog and mixed-signal models must be manually translated into schematics and further developed using specialized AMS design flows. In case detailed transient simulations are required, available AMS models must be replaced by equivalent transistor-level models that can be verified by circuit simulators such as PSPICE. The expected outcome of this phase is a circuit layout for a printed circuit board.

Embedded software may be already adequate for its implementation in a microcontroller or DSP. However, it may also be the case that it requires further development, in which case it is handed over to specialized design flow tools that provide further design capabilities. Typical IDEs used for this purpose are IAR Embedded Workbench [67], Code Composer Studio [126] and µVision [8]. The expected outcome is an executable binary file compiled for a specific instruction set architecture.

5.2.5 Implementation

Hardware, software, analog and mixed-signal components of an embedded system are brought together in the integration phase for the construction of a first hardware prototype. Experimental setups are also constructed in test laboratories equipped with appropriate test equipment. Within this stage, design iterations on hardware prototypes must be performed to correct possible design errors.

The structure of a hardware prototype in terms of HW/SW and AMS components at this point is very similar to the one used in a final product. Further tests which are not shown in Figure 5.1 are performed afterward for certification purposes. More details regarding the type of certification tests required for industrial instruments can be found in [113].

5.3 Structure of a virtual prototype

The integrated design flow described above suggests the use of system level modeling for enhancing available design verification capabilities. It provides embedded system designers with an efficient modeling and simulation infrastructure to identify and solve design flaws earlier in a design stage, allowing further decisions to be tested as many times as required. Such tests can be performed in a very short time span and can help verify a design without the need of hardware prototypes and experimental setups.

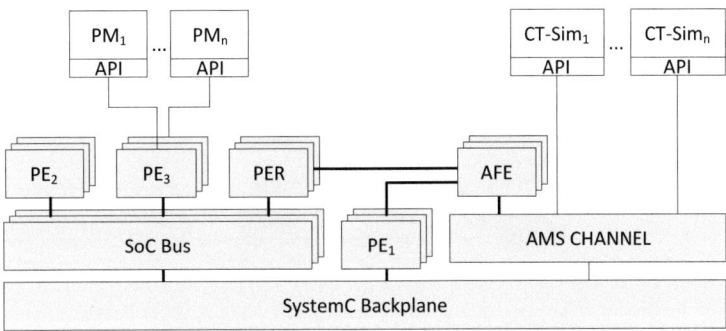

Figure 5.4: Meta-structure of a virtual prototype

Eventually, the end goal of the proposed system modeling stage is to help improve the confidence in a design, avoiding costly and time consuming redesign cycles in the implementation phase.

A system level design methodology must indicate how the design goals described above can be achieved in an efficient manner. Such a methodology must initially specify how models are constructed and afterward tested according to a series of verification goals. This section describes the guidelines for the creation of system level models. Chapter 6 describes a problem-oriented verification strategy for system level models.

The meta-structure of a virtual prototype is shown in Figure 5.4. A virtual prototype is created as an instance of such meta-structure. The term meta-structure was adopted from the definition of meta-models [103], which refers to them as models of the structure of models. The meta-structure describes the allowed components and interconnections in a virtual prototype. Each block represents a component from either the physical or digital domain (hardware and software). The allowed components are: Processing Elements (PE), Peripherals (PER), system-on-chip (SoC) buses, Analog and Mixed-Signal (AMS) channels and Analog Front Ends (AFE).

All components listed above are modeled as SystemC module classes and are able to communicate with each other via ports and TLM-2.0 interfaces. Their behavior may be described natively using SystemC processes or via external simulators. Two types of external simulators are allowed: instruction set simulators or emulators for Processor Models (PM) and continuous-time simulators (CT-Sim) for AMS models.

The SystemC backplane from Figure 5.4 corresponds to a SystemC top module from which all other components are instantiated. The SystemC backplane is able to control the simulation of the complete platform, making it the simulation master, or may yield control to other simulators, making it a simulation slave. Further implementation details on this topic are presented in Chapter 7.

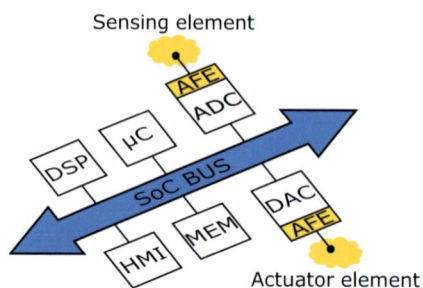

Figure 5.5: Instance of a virtual prototype

Components from the meta-structure can be instantiated as many times as required with the exception of the AMS Channel which can only be instantiated once. These instances are used to construct a virtual prototype. Thus, a virtual prototype is consistent as long as it follows the interconnection scheme defined by the meta-structure.

An example of a virtual prototype instance is shown in Figure 5.5. The virtual prototype is a system level model of an heterogeneous system with two Processing Elements (a microcontroller and a DSP), one SoC bus, four Peripherals (HMI, memory, DAC and ADC) and two Analog Front Ends (used to connect ADC and DAC peripherals to sensing and actuating elements, respectively). The behavior of the sensing and actuating elements is described by some continuous-time simulator.

5.3.1 Processing elements

Three types of processing elements are defined and can be instantiated as many times as required in a virtual prototype. They are hardware models of software programmable components (DSP and microcontroller architectures) and hardware programmable components (custom FPGA architectures). Their behavior is described by C/C++ based embedded software in the form of a tasks and Interrupt Service Routine functions.

Figure 5.6 shows the structure of the three available processing elements PE_x. The basic elements of functionality are tasks T_x and interrupt service routines ISR_x. The basic communication elements between tasks and interrupt service routines are channels c_x.

PE_1 and PE_2 processing elements

The structure of PE_1 and PE_2 elements is shown in Figures 5.6a and 5.6b respectively. They are declared as native SystemC modules. PE_1 and PE_2 elements are equivalent in

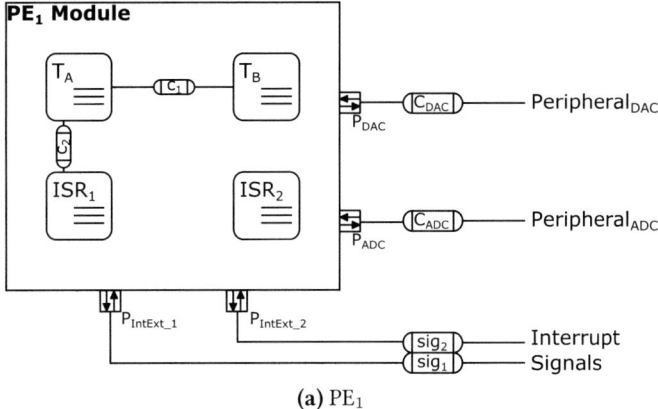

(a) PE$_1$

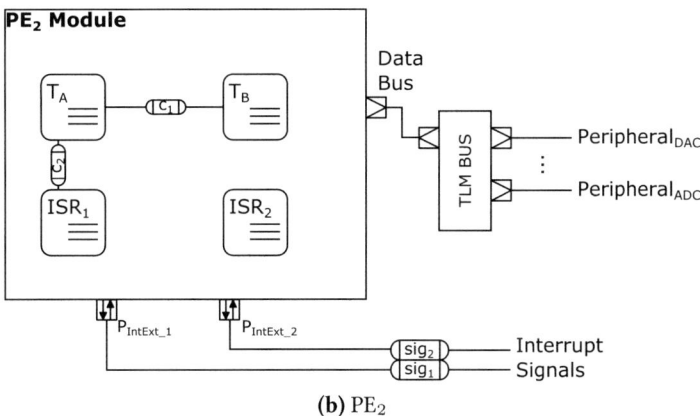

(b) PE$_2$

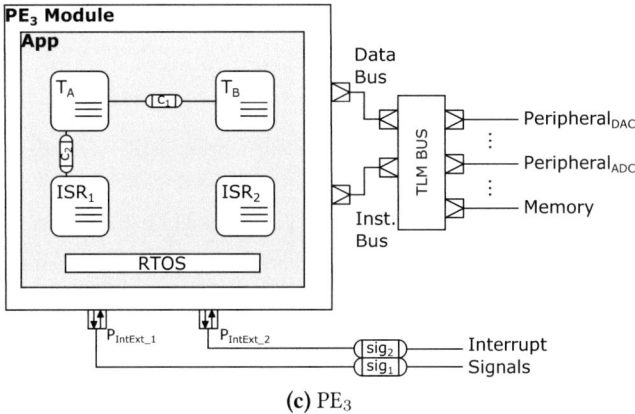

(c) PE$_3$

Figure 5.6: Structure of available processing elements

terms of their processing capabilities. Tasks are declared as SystemC processes. Interrupt service routines are declared as SystemC methods sensitive to events on interrupt ports P_{IntExt_x}. Channels are declared as shared variables or as semaphores from SystemC primitive channel mechanisms.

PE_1 and PE_2 elements are approximately-timed models with no micro-architectural descriptions. Time annotation is done manually via SystemC *wait()* function calls inside tasks and interrupt service routines. More advanced time annotation techniques such as automated source-level code annotation [116] are not currently supported, but could be implemented.

The difference between PE_1 and PE_2 elements are their external communication interfaces. PE_1 elements use traditional SystemC ports to communicate with external primitive channels. PE_2 elements can also use traditional SystemC ports, but they can additionally use TLM interfaces for communicating with TLM compatible hierarchical channels.

PE_3 processing elements

The structure of a PE$_3$ element is shown in Figure 5.6c. A PE$_3$ element is declared as native SystemC modules, but its functionality is declared outside SystemC. This is possible since PE$_3$ elements act as wrappers for encapsulating the functionality of processor models PM_x executing on external simulators. The shaded block in Figure 5.6c represents a cross-complied embedded software application. Therefore, functionality is described using embedded software which is cross-compiled for a particular micro-controller architecture. The functional elements and internal communication elements available depend on the mechanisms supported by the selected RTOS.

The processor models from PE$_3$ elements use emulation technologies to execute binary source code for specific microprocessor or DSP instruction sets. They may be instruction- or cycle-accurate, depending on their underlying technology. Their simulators have high performance (tens or hundreds of MIPS) in comparison to interpreted instruction set simulators and are available in the commercial and academic domains. Time advances in fixed steps of time called quantum. The amount of assembly instructions a simulator can execute per quantum depends on the type of simulator (instruction- or cycle-accurate) and on the processor speed, which is typically a constant parameter throughout a simulation.

PE_3 elements are allowed to communicate using SystemC ports and TLM interfaces. The access to these ports and interfaces is done via callback functions declared inside the PE_3 SystemC module. These callback functions route incoming and outgoing communication requests from an external processor model to their respective SystemC port or TLM interface.

5.3.2 SoC buses

The communication between digital components is handled via a system-on-chip (SoC) bus. Whenever a processor requires performing read/write operations on registers belonging to peripherals or save/load information to external memories, it does so by accessing their associated address in the memory map. Such requests are handled by a bus model and are assigned payloads which include some of the attributes found in typical memory-mapped bus protocols (command, address, data, byte enables, single word transfers, burst transfers, streaming, and response status [70]).

Bus models are provided with multiple TLM-2.0 target and initiator socket interfaces used to route read/write communication requests. They are shown in Figure 5.6 as the components labeled TLM BUS.

The communicant functionality of SoC buses are defined inside SystemC hierarchical channels. Their complexity may vary from simple loosely-timed bus models that implement the default payload from the TLM standard [70] and up to cycle-accurate models such as the AMBA bus model [27].

5.3.3 Peripherals

Peripheral models are system level models containing structural and behavioral descriptions of embedded system components such as memories, digital and analog I/O modules, serial interfaces, external timers, interrupt controllers, etc. In terms of their structure, they are modeled as SystemC modules with TLM-2.0 interfaces for memory-mapped communication and simple output ports for interrupt triggering capabilities. Peripheral models are provided with a TLM-2.0 target socket interface used to respond to read-/write communication requests. The way in which processors, buses and peripherals interconnect via TLM-2.0 interfaces in a virtual prototype can be inferred from Figure 3.8, where processor models act as initiators, buses as interconnects and peripherals as targets.

All TLM-2.0 based communication in a virtual prototype is done via a memory-mapped bus model that mimic the way in which communication is performed in real embedded systems. They are accessed via memory-mapped registers, as in real embedded systems, thus available software drivers can be reused by the processing elements that communicate with them. In memory-mapped communication, register addresses

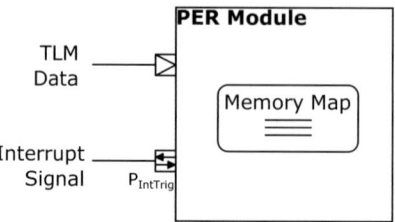

Figure 5.7: Peripheral model

belonging to peripherals and addresses belonging to external memories are associated to a processor's memory map. A memory map contains the range of addresses accessible to a processor, such as addresses for the processor's internal memory space and control registers, as well as addresses mapped to peripherals' registers and external memories.

Their functionality of peripheral models is modeled based on technical specifications available from IC providers or as custom components describing hardware accelerators in FPGA implementations. Behavioral models describe the functionality of peripherals whenever read or write requests are performed on address spaces owed by them. In addition, behavioral descriptions are allowed to include timing information regarding the communication and execution of behavioral descriptions. For instance, an external memory model may indicate the amount of time a processor must wait after requesting a load or store operation on it. Such timing information can be added via SystemC *wait()* function calls.

5.3.4 AMS channel

An AMS Channel acts as a coordinator between SystemC and external continuous-time simulators (CT-Sim) for AMS models. It contains a set of coordination laws, namely co-simulation schemes that specify how external simulators are initialized, parametrized, controlled and terminated, and how data and time are synchronized. Any number of CT simulators can be connected to an AMS Channel, as shown in Figure 5.4, as long as they provide suitable API function for control and data synchronization. Most commercial CT simulators provide such API functions, e.g. SMASH from Dolpin Integration, Saber from Synopsis, MATLAB /Simulink from Mathworks, Allegro from Cadence, LTspice from Linear Technologies.

Channels are developed as SystemC wrappers where co-simulation schemes are implemented. Deriving such schemes requires an expert knowledge of the underlying models of computation and their simulator engines. Further implementation details on this topic are presented in Chapter 7.

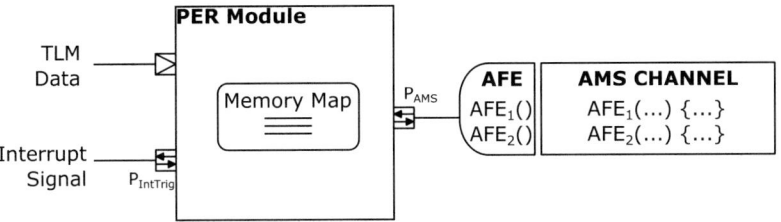

Figure 5.8: Peripheral model with connection to an AFE

5.3.5 Analog Front Ends

Peripherals that require communication with an external continuous-time simulator must be connected to an AFE for enabling data compatibility. They are I/O peripherals such as ADC, DAC, GPIO and interrupt controllers, which in the real world are in contact with physical processes.

AFE models are developed as SystemC interfaces that connect to AMS Channels as shown in Figure 5.8. The behavior of an AFE model is described by the AMS Channel it is attached to. Such behavior defines simple data conversion activities such as quantization and encapsulating of data into compatible data types. Moreover, AFE models of ADC and DAC peripherals can be linked to AMS channels that define additional data conversion parameters such as conversion gain, single-ended or differential I/O, digital format, among others. Further data conversion parameters can be added based on technical data-sheets of I/O peripherals.

6

Design Methodology and Problem-Oriented Verification

This chapter describes a system level design methodology and a problem-oriented verification approach based on virtual prototyping. It is applicable throughout initial design stages and up to the implementation of a system in hardware prototypes and experimental setups. It also allows for top-down or bottom-up verification approaches in order to target specific verification goals. The methodology suggests a series modeling and simulation activities that can be performed at different design stages and their expected outcome. It enables the verification a design in various stages to evaluate the impact that different design decisions may have on it. Most importantly, it enables efficient means to detect and solve problems that may occur during different states of the design of embedded systems.

6.1 Design and verification methodology

This section proposes a problem-oriented design and verification approach based on the creation of simulation models for identifying and solving design problems during the development process of embedded systems. The abstraction levels in which models are described are defined according to a set of verification goals related to specific design problems.

6.1.1 Modeling abstractions

The key aspect of any model-based design approach is finding the right modeling language and abstraction in order to solve particular design challenges. Figure 6.1 shows the main abstraction layers for constructing virtual prototypes. The digital domain contains models of embedded system components such as microcontrollers, buses, memories, AD and DA converters, interrupt controllers and other common peripherals. They are constructed using SystemC and OVP models. The physical domain contains models of analog front-ends (AFE) from embedded systems, such as passive and active electronic components, and physical plant models coming from different domains. They are constructed using MATLAB Simulink and VHDL-AMS models. All these models and their native simulators can be seamlessly coupled by the co-simulation framework described in Chapter 7 in order to obtain the behavior of full systems.

Layers A, B and C from Figure 6.1 correspond to incremental refinements on the structure and behavior of a virtual prototype. The verification goals for each layer are different and depend on the development stage. Design activities start with a high abstraction in order to obtain outputs that can be verified according to specifications in a very short time span. Further steps require the addition of more details into designs related to their implementation; each step also providing outputs for verification purposes.

The design must not necessary follow a top-down approach. It can also follow a bottom-up approach to target specific verification goals. Each layer can be implemented independently and scaled according to the verification goals explained in the following sections. Any abstraction in between the three main defined abstractions is valid as long as it follows the modeling guidelines described in Section 5.3. Therefore, embedded system developers are also free to implement any of these layers independently and scale them according to particular design challenges or verification goals.

6.1.2 Concept-Oriented virtual prototype

A SW Stack is defined as a hardware independent implementation developed in C/C++ that describes the functionality of an application that will later on be executed in an embedded system. It typically describes signal processing and control algorithms implemented manually or generated automatically from higher-level modes of state charts and data flow models.

The SW Stack is mapped to a PE_1 element. In order for it to interact with the physical domain and vice versa, read/write functions from an AMS Channel serving as I/O interface are available. Data going in and out the physical domain must pass

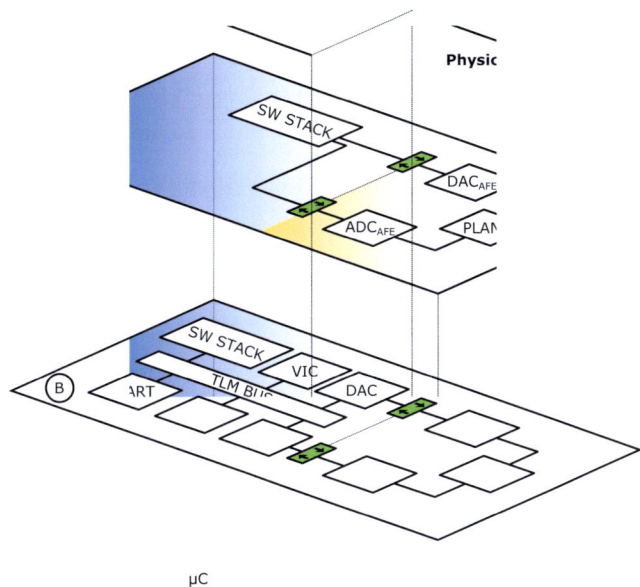

Figure 6.1: Virtual prototype abstraction layers: *(A)* Concept-Oriented, *(B)* Architecture-Oriented, *(C)* Implementation-Oriented

through DAC and ADC Analog Front Ends (AFE) respectively. The model complexity of the physical domain can be as complex as required, e.g. a plant described as a transfer function with noise disturbances and an AFE as a Sigma-Delta converter.

Verification goals

The verification goal on this level is the correct SW stack application functionality. Common problems that can be identified are the incorrect implementation of control or signal processing algorithms and deadlocks. Initial studies on the influence of noise and distortions from the physical process on the SW stack can be carried out. Since the SW Stack can also include estimates of timing behavior, its influence on the physical process can be observed. The advantage of this level of modeling abstraction is high simulation speed, thus a wide range of scenarios can be easily simulated.

Design activities	Test activities
• Partition between digital and AMS systems • Separation of activities into tasks and define means for communicating between them (semaphores, mutex, FIFOs, shared variables) • Determine number of analog and digital I/O ports needed for a PE • Determine number of interrupts needed and create respective ISR functions	• Test fixed-point or floating point implementation of algorithms • Determine effects of quantization • Test influence of noise sources on signal processing algorithms • Determine effects of sampling rate • Perform scripted Monte Carlo style analysis

Timing and task scheduling	Verification goals
• Specify time passing according to cyclic tasks. No performance information can be obtained, all are estimates. • Non-preemptive scheduling of tasks done by SystemC scheduler	• Verify functionality of signal processing algorithms • Verify the robustness of algorithms in noisy and fault prone scenarios

Table 6.1: Concept-Oriented virtual prototype

Table 6.1 provides a summary of the design, test and verification activities supported by Concept-Oriented virtual prototypes.

6.1.3 Architecture-Oriented virtual prototype

An architecture-oriented virtual prototype has a clear separation between communication and computation components. In this case, a SW stack is mapped to a PE_2 element. Computation is done by the SW stack, and communication to peripherals is done via device drivers that access memory mapped I/O addresses. Peripherals are allowed to request polling from the SW stack via interrupt driven I/Os that trigger ISR calls in the SW Stack. Communication details are completely hidden to the SW Stack and are handled by a SoC Bus model. An architecture-oriented virtual prototype closely resembles HW and SW components of a real embedded system. Therefore, embedded software and drivers can be created or reused from available legacy code.

I/O peripherals such as a VIC (Vector Interrupt Controller: the term is taken from ARM architectural descriptions), GPIO, UART, ADC and DAC are added along with a SoC bus model, as shown in Figure 6.1. Functionality of peripherals is modeled based on technical specification available from IC providers. Typically, an engineer does not need to model the complete functionality of a peripheral, thus the modeling effort is low. Additionally, SW drivers for each peripheral must be created to simplify the development of embedded software in the SW Stack.

Function calls to the co-simulation API are removed from the SW Stack and are placed in ADC and DAC peripherals. A SW Stack will now have access to I/O data from the physical domain via SW drivers that access ADC and DAC components. Additionally, due to the use of SystemC and TLM 2.0 standards, timing behavior estimates of the SW Stack, bus transfers and I/O peripherals can be included in the models.

Verification goals

The verification goal on this level is the functionality of the communication layer. It provides visibility on the bus and the transactions between the SW stack and peripherals. Typical problems that can be identified are communication bottlenecks caused by a high number of calls to certain peripherals. SW drivers can be developed and tested at this point. Since the digital model also contains estimates for processing and communication times, their influence on the physical process and vice versa can be observed on simulation traces.

Table 6.2 provides a summary of the design, test and verification activities supported by Architecture-Oriented virtual prototypes.

6.1.4 Implementation-Oriented virtual prototype

In an implementation-oriented virtual prototype, the SW Stack is assigned to a PE_3 element. The SW Stack contains application and hardware dependent software compiled for a specific instruction set architecture. A processor emulator is able to efficiently execute the binary code in an instruction-accurate manner. The same code can be later on executed by a real processor.

The reason for constructing such complex embedded system models is because they are able to execute unmodified production level code compiled for a specific instruction set architecture. This makes it possible to simulate compiled code which provides

Design activities	Test activities
• HW/SW partitioning • Model peripheral models and develop their corresponding drivers • Define how digital communication is done (payload) • Define peripheral memory map • Define peripheral pooling mechanisms	• Determine required communication throughput • Test complex communication buses • Monitor bus activity and find bottlenecks

Timing and task scheduling	Verification goals
• Specify time passing according to cyclic tasks. No performance information can be obtained, all are estimates. • Non-preemptive scheduling of tasks done by SystemC scheduler	• Verify functionality of device drivers • Verify functionality of hardware dependent communication stacks

Table 6.2: Architecture-Oriented virtual prototype

approximate-timing information regarding the performance of a real embedded system. In addition, the simulation performance of such virtual prototype is orders of magnitude higher than cycle-accurate ISS and VHDL models.

An implementation-oriented virtual prototype provides the necessary HW infrastructure to natively support the execution of an RTOS inside the microcontroller module. However, it is often the case that the memory mapped address space of the HW infrastructure does not match exactly that of an available RTOS, in which case porting effort is required. SystemC constructs that were used in the SW Stack of an architecture-oriented virtual prototype, such as semaphores, queues, and timed delays, are typically supported by any RTOS. Therefore, the advantage of using an RTOS is a straightforward translation of the SW Stack to a specific RTOS implementation. SystemC is no longer used for scheduling and execution of the embedded software. Instead, an RTOS specific scheduler is used to natively execute computations.

Design activities	Test activities
• Execute native binary code • Develop hardware dependent software functions • Port available hardware dependent legacy code	• Debug native instructions of an instruction set • Determine the effects of interrupt priorities and interrupt nesting • Determine the effects of task priorities (priority inversion) • Memory footprint analysis (stack, heap)

Timing and task scheduling	Verification goals
• Passing of time according to assembly instructions being executed. Provides instruction-accurate timing information for profiling. • Preemptive scheduling of tasks	• Verify hardware dependent software • Verify RTOS implementation

Table 6.3: Implementation-Oriented virtual prototype

Verification goals

The verification goals on this level are the RTOS integration and the full system functionality. It is particularly useful to understand the complex interaction between the physical domain and an RTOS. Common problems that can be identified are stack overflows and priority inversion problems. Since the embedded software is already complied for a specific microcontroller architecture, metrics for a HW implementation such as memory footprint of an RTOS and its embedded software are easily obtained. Estimate performance metrics can also be obtained, however they must be interpreted with care since various factors can lead to high inaccuracies. Such considerations are: (1) dynamic effects of pipeline and cache are not considered by a processor emulator and (2) timing for peripherals and bus delays depend on the correctness of the estimates given by an engineer.

Table 6.3 provides a summary of the design, test and verification activities supported by Implementation-Oriented virtual prototypes.

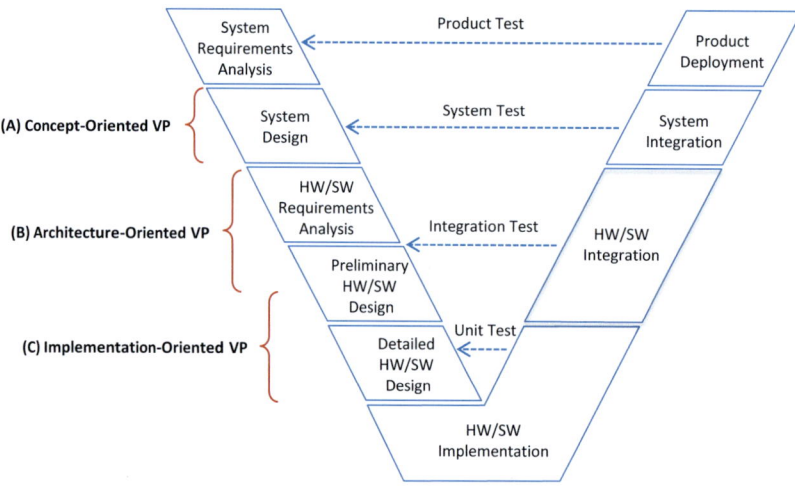

Figure 6.2: Virtual prototypes in the V-Model

6.2 Support for the development life-cycle

The advantage of the problem-oriented design methodology described above relies in the fact that it can be implemented at any point of an embedded system development cycle; specifically where design problems need to be identified and solved. The methodology suggests the use of additional modeling and simulation tools which have a low implementation effort. Designers may opt to use them according to design problems and their verification goals.

Figure 6.2 shows the main abstraction layers for constructing multi-domain virtual prototypes and the design stages, according to the V-Model, in which they can be used. Multi-domain virtual prototypes provide valuable support for testing activities throughout a the development life-cycle as shown in the V-Model. The advantages of adopting virtual prototypes in a development process are:

1. Support the current design stage by providing multi-domain system level simulation models with tracing, debugging and profiling capabilities

2. Test normal operation and fault condition scenarios in a simulation environment without the need of hardware prototypes and experimental setups

3. Support integration and test activities according to the V-model by providing reference models for unit, integration and system tests

6.2.1 System tests

A concept-oriented virtual prototype can be used as a reference for system tests. System tests are intended to verify the full behavior of a system. They require testing normal and fault condition scenarios which would be otherwise impossible with real hardware prototypes and experimental setups. These scenarios can be reproduced in simulations and efficiently tested together with a concept-oriented virtual prototype.

The high abstraction in which concept-oriented virtual prototypes are developed make it possible to test in a very short time scenarios which might not be feasible in real life. Most of these scenarios deal with the uncertainties that physical models introduce in embedded systems.

6.2.2 Integration tests

An architecture-oriented virtual prototype defines the structure of HW/SW and AMS components of a system. It provides an efficient way to specify and test communication requirements between components. For example, it provides means for specifying the payload used for a digital communication protocol, the polling rate for a peripheral, the sequence required for a device driver to read data from a peripheral, the behavior of an Interrupt Service Routine, etc. The advantage of having such virtual prototype is that it can be used as reference for integration tests.

A way to perform integration tests is to reuse test scenarios that were used to test an architecture-oriented virtual platform. Therefore, the integration test goal is to verify that results obtained from a hardware prototype and experimental setup comply with those specified by the architecture-oriented virtual prototype.

6.2.3 Unit tests

During unit tests, individual software applications are tested with respect to their interface definition using module test functions. The goal is to verify their correct internal object handling and behavior. An implementation-oriented virtual prototype can be used for performing unit-tests when a hardware implementation is not available. Such virtual prototypes are able to execute native binary code in an instruction-accurate manner, which is enough for unit-testing purposes. Thus, unit tests executed in an implementation-oriented virtual prototype will behave the same way as it would do in a hardware implementation.

Software applications that make use of hardware-dependent software (see Figure 2.8) can also be subject for unit testing in an implementation-oriented virtual prototype. This is possible since virtual prototypes contain functional models of hardware. These models are typically peripheral models that respond to requests generated by software applications. It must be taken into consideration that such hardware models are commonly simplified models providing basic functionalities. Therefore, testing hardware-dependent software that requires complex interactions with hardware components might not always be possible.

The benefit of performing unit-testing in an implementation-oriented virtual prototype is that testing can be performed before a hardware prototype is available. However, unit testing can only be as reliable as the models that compose the virtual prototype. This means that all models used must have been validated together with their real counterparts. Processor models available from EDA commercial suppliers are validated and reliable models. This is not the case for peripheral models, which must be manually modeled and validated. The implementation effort is initially high, but as more components are added to a library and reused in other projects, the effort decreases.

7

Co-Simulation Framework

This chapter describes the co-simulation framework used by the virtual prototypes and verification methodology described in this work. The co-simulation algorithm developed for this purpose is described and its implementation for coupling the following simulation engines: SystemC/Simulink and SystemC/SMASH. In both cases, the modeling and simulation capabilities inherent to each tool were not affected. A configuration management software is also described, which eases the effort of interconnecting models pertaining to different simulators and helps configure available debugging, tracing and profiling mechanisms.

7.1 Overview

The co-simulation framework described in this chapter is shown in Figure 7.1. It is the result of coupling specialized simulation tools for HW/SW co-design of embedded systems and simulation tools for multi-domain physical systems. Its simulation engine relies of Discrete-Event (DE) simulators for embedded systems models and Continuous-Time (CT) simulators for multi-physical domain models. The coupling is done with a DE/CT co-simulation algorithm that defines the necessary control and communication semantics.

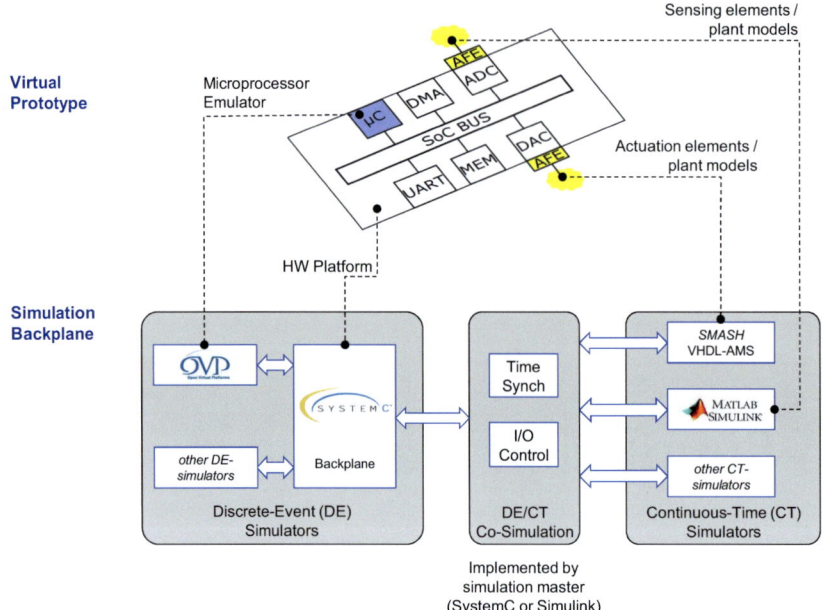

Figure 7.1: Co-simulation framework for virtual prototypes

7.1.1 Supported modeling and simulation tools

The modeling and simulation tools used in this work were selected according to best-practices in the industrial automation domain. MATLAB/Simulink and the SMASH [40] simulator for VHDL-AMS were selected as CT simulators. Both simulators provide effective means for describing physical systems. In addition, these simulators already form part of current design practices in the industrial automation domain. This is especially true in case of Simulink, which has been for many years a de-facto tool for algorithmic modeling and simulation.

SystemC was selected as DE simulator since it provides useful means for describing hardware and software components of embedded systems. SystemC suggests a promising implementation future in the industrial automation domain. According to current research publications, SystemC is already used for embedded system design in R&D activities in companies such as ABB [101], Siemens [53] and Bosch [66, 77, 78].

The commercial emulation tool Open Virtual Platforms (OVP) [73] from Imperas was selected as de-facto emulator for processor models of embedded systems. This implied no additional adaption effort to the co-simulation algorithms described in this chapter since all OVP models are provided with SystemC wrappers. This means that the execution of

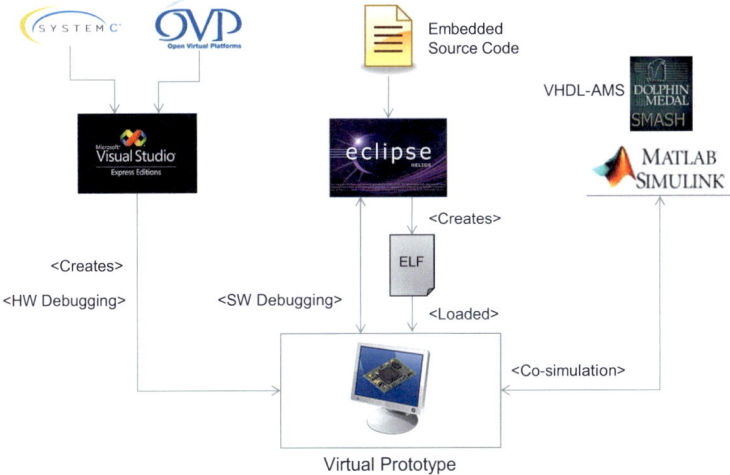

Figure 7.2: Tool flow used for construction, debugging and co-simulation of virtual proto-types

OVP processor models is encapsulated by wrappers, which are subsequently controlled by the SystemC scheduler. Therefore, the execution of OVP processor models can be directly controlled through the SystemC scheduler.

7.1.2 Tool flow description

Figure 7.2 describes the tool flow used for the construction, debugging and co-simulation of virtual prototypes. A virtual prototype is constructed using libraries and DLLs from SystemC and OVP processor emulation tool. The Microsoft Visual Studio C++ development environment is used for creating and debugging hardware aspects of a virtual prototype. Embedded software code is developed in an Eclipse IDE and complied/linked with a GCC cross-compilation tool chain. GDB is used for debugging software applications loaded into a virtual prototype. This is possible thanks to a built-in GDB server in the OVP processor emulation tool. Finally, the co-simulation between digital components of embedded systems and multi-domain physical models is done between SystemC and the continuous-time simulators MATLAB /Simulink and SMASH.

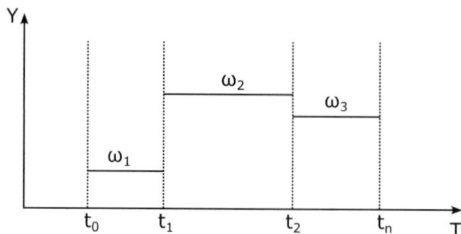

Figure 7.3: Piecewise constant segments

7.2 Modeling formalisms and their simulators

DE and CT simulators have been long studied in modeling and simulation theory [138]. A review of their underlying models of computation is presented ahead. This information will be afterward used to infer their co-simulation semantics.

7.2.1 Discrete-Event (DE) simulation

Models of the digital domain operate on a discrete time basis with outputs that are piecewise constant function of time as illustrated in Figure 7.3. In DE simulators, time advances according to scheduled events stored inside the simulator's event queue. Each event is assigned to a time-stamp that defines the future point in simulation time in which it will be executed. Each time an event is executed, all processes sensitive to the event are executed. This may lead to changes in the event queue, i.e. new events can be notified and existing ones can be rescheduled or canceled.

The hardware simulators VHDL, Verilog and SystemC are examples of DE simulators. Hardware simulators use additionally the notion of delta-cycles to simulate conceptually concurrent processes. A finite number of delta-cycles is allowed to execute in the current time step t_c without increasing simulation time. A delta-cycle is allowed to finish after all events scheduled for the current time step t_c have been executed, i.e. there are no events marked with t_c inside the event queue. Afterwards, simulation time is allowed to advance to the next scheduled event t_n, equivalent to the first event in the event queue. This is followed by the execution of the event inside a new delta-cycle. The following conclusion is obtained:

Definition 7.1. In a DE simulation, the *next time step t_n* is obtained by examining the simulator's event queue after the last delta of a current time step t_c has been executed.

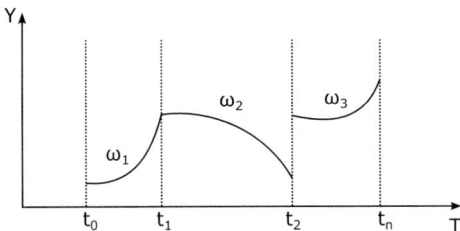

Figure 7.4: Piecewise continuous segments

7.2.2 Continuous-Time (CT) simulation

Models of the physical domain are described using sets of simultaneous differential and algebraic equations that are piecewise continuous functions of time as illustrated in Figure 7.4. CT simulators are used to obtain the behavior of continuous dynamic systems expressed in terms of differential and algebraic equations. The heart of any CT simulator is a numerical integration method that discretizes differential equations and transform them into difference equations that can be solved by a computer.

A variety of numerical integrations are available and classified as fixed-step or variable-step solvers. Fixed-step simulators perform numerical integration on fixed integration steps which must be carefully selected according to the application. A too big integration step might lead to inaccuracies or even unstable behavior, while a too small integration step will lead to very long computation times. Most importantly, fixed-step solvers are not able to accurately detect zero-crossings required for DE/CT co-simulation. Therefore, fixed-step solvers are not adequate for DE/CT co-simulation and are not considered in this work.

On the other hand, variable-step solvers automatically adapt the integration time step according to the behavior of a system. Figure 7.5a shows how a variable step solver decreases the simulation step size h_n to increase accuracy when continuous states change rapidly. The solver increases the step size up to h_{max} when continuous states change slowly in order to save simulation time. Variable step solvers are chosen for DE/CT co-simulation since they are efficient, provide accurate results and can locate zero-crossing in an accurate manner. Most commercial CT simulators implement variable step solvers, e.g. PSPICE electric circuit simulators, Simulink and SMASH.

Discontinuities in dynamic systems are specified using conditions such as thresholds. When these conditions are fulfilled, they change the dynamic behavior of the system. Zero-crossing detection mechanisms are a way to specify and detect such conditions. A zero-crossing detector determines the exact simulation time a continuous variable

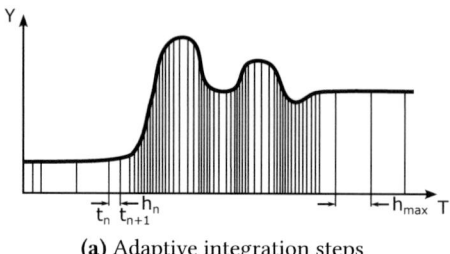

(a) Adaptive integration steps

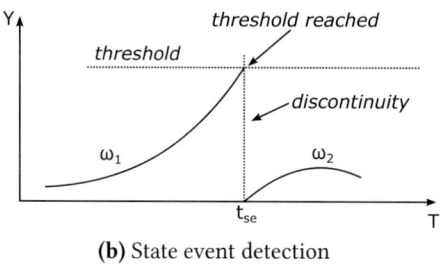

(b) State event detection

Figure 7.5: Capabilities of CT simulators

crosses the vertical axis (the offset of the vertical axis can be adapted for specifying a threshold). A zero-crossing detector relies on a bisection algorithm that adapts the integration step until the crossing is detected with a defined accuracy. For example, in Figure 7.5b, a discontinuity is specified whenever $f_1(t)$ crosses a defined threshold value. Once this happens, a zero-crossing detector will find the time of the crossing, which afterward trigger a state event. A state event specifies a new dynamic behavior of the system, in this case, as a new set of equations which must now be solved to obtain the behavior $f_2(t)$. Therefore, a state event is defined as:

Definition 7.2. In CT simulation, a *state event* produces a discontinuity in the dynamic behavior of a system. It is triggered when a condition on a continuous variable, e.g. a threshold, becomes true.

7.3 DE/CT co-simulation

A generic DE/CT co-simulation scheme is presented ahead. It is generic since it is based on the operation principles of DE and CT simulators, regardless of their implementation by a specific simulator. Further in this chapter, its implementation is described for coupling the DE simulator SystemC with the CT simulators Simulink and Smash. In both cases, the generic DE/CT co-simulation scheme presented ahead was followed.

The proposed approach is intended to couple a DE simulator to multiple CT simulators in a *one-to-many* approach as shown in Figure 7.6. It relies on a simulation coordinator responsible for executing the control and communication semantics of the co-simulation scheme. The location of the coordinator influences the implementation of the co-simulation scheme, but it does not alter the semantics of the co-simulation. The co-simulation scheme shares the same operation principles as the simulation cycles of DEV&DESS [138] and VHDL-AMS [30]. However, the proposed approach is not intended to execute inside a single framework. Instead, the proposed DE/CT co-simulation approach is designed to coordinate the simulation of multiple models interconnected between each other and distributed among multiple simulation frameworks. A further advantage is that the debugging and visualization capabilities of the simulation frameworks being coupled are not affected. This is intended to increase the acceptance of co-simulation among embedded system developers by providing extensions to commonly used simulation frameworks rather than providing a complete new set of tools. The flexibility provided by this approach is essential when multiple domain-specific languages are used for the design of embedded systems.

7.3.1 Principles of simulation coupling

Co-simulation is a common approach for addressing the heterogeneity of models whose behavior can otherwise not be obtained by a single simulation engine. This is the case for applications such as embedded control systems and cyber-physical or hybrid systems where the digital and physical domains are tightly coupled and cannot be tested in separation.

A co-simulation scheme defines the interoperation semantics for control and communication required for coupling two or more simulation engines. The execution of a co-simulation scheme is assigned to an entity called *coordinator*. A coordinator can be a software application running as an independent process (Figure 7.6c) or it can be embedded into one of the simulation engines (Figures 7.6a and 7.6b). A coordinator is responsible for executing the control and communication semantics defined by the co-simulation scheme.

The *control semantics* define how simulators are executed and how their simulation time is allowed to advance. The execution of multiple simulators may be done through their alternate or parallel execution. Most importantly, the control semantics specify

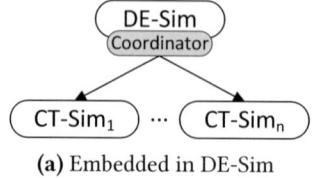

(a) Embedded in DE-Sim

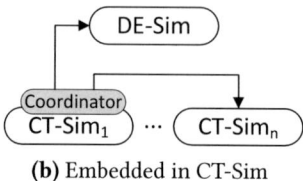

(b) Embedded in CT-Sim

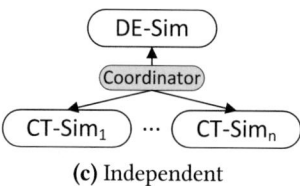

(c) Independent

Figure 7.6: Examples of coordinators for a DE/CT co-simulation

how time advances in each simulator, that is, how and up to which point each simulator is allowed to execute or interrupt its own execution.

On the other hand, the *communication semantics* specify how and when information must be shared between simulation engines. Communication is done through application programming interfaces (APIs) connected via 1 such as shared memory or TCP/IP. Most importantly, the communication semantics define when and what type of information must be transferred between simulators in order for them to interoperate in an efficient and coherent manner.

The effort involved in creating and implementing a co-simulation scheme is considerable. Such effort can be reduced if a generic co-simulation scheme is initially devised based on the operation principles of the simulators involved. These principles are also called models of computation. Such scheme can be implemented afterward for all simulators that follow the same models of computation. The work of Zeigler [138] and Lee[83] demonstrates that only a handful of models of computation are in fact needed to describe almost any simulation engine. Therefore, when elaborating new co-simulation schemes, it is convenient to focus on the underlying models of computation of the simulation engines involved, rather than on the specific details of each simulator.

7.3.2 Implementation requirements

The implementation of the DE/CT co-simulation scheme described in Section 7.3 is done inside a program entity called coordinator. A coordinator (refer to Figure 7.6) is a set of functions embedded into one of the involved simulators or an independent application running as an external process. The location of the coordinator does not affect the principles of the co-simulation. Instead, it defines the technical details of the implementation, e.g. the APIs and middleware used to communicate and control simulators.

The requirements for selecting appropriate DE and CT simulators for DE/CT co-simulation are:

1. All DE and CT simulators selected must be either flexible enough to support the embedding of a coordinator or provide appropriate APIs to control them by an external coordinator.

2. The requirements for a DE simulator are:

    2.1. Provide event introspection capabilities. This means that the event queue of the simulator can be consulted at any point of the simulation.

    2.2. Provide means to detect the last delta-cycle of a current time step.

    2.3. Be able to execute up to desired points in simulation time and resume execution afterwards.

3. The requirements for a CT simulator are:

    3.1. Its simulation engine must rely on any type of variable-step numerical integration methods.

    3.2. Provide zero-crossing mechanisms to detect with precision discontinuities in models.

    3.3. Be able to execute up to desired points in simulation time and resume execution afterward.

7.3.3 Simulation cycle

The semantics of the DE/CT co-simulation scheme are informally described in order to be understood by most readers, i.e. engineers and physicists familiar with simulation frameworks for digital and physical systems. Figure 7.7 is used to describe the DE/CT co-simulation cycle:

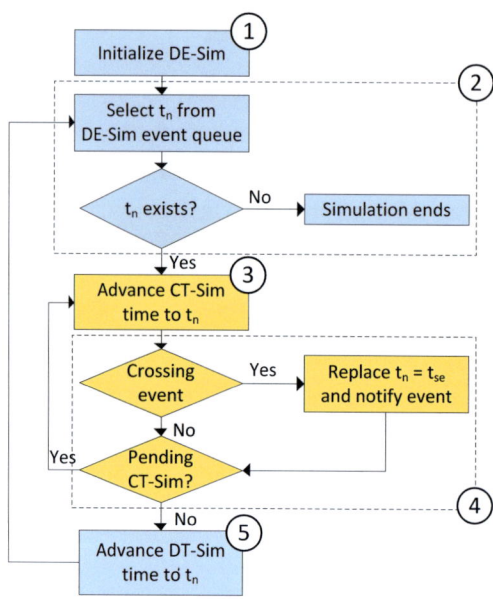

Figure 7.7: DE/CT co-simulation cycle

1. The coordinator indicates the DE-Sim to initialize which will trigger the execution of its internal processes until they yield. The event queue is now populated with time events.

2. The coordinator looks into the DE-Sim event queue and determines the next synchronization point t_n (refer to Definition 7.1). It determines t_n after filtering the DE-Sim event queue in order to find scheduled events that require synchronization with CT simulators. Since all events are endowed with the name of their owner process, the coordinator uses this information to identify them. This requires registering the name of such processes to the coordinator before simulation starts. Not doing so would imply forcing unneeded synchronization points which would considerably decrease simulation performance.

3. The coordinator is responsible for triggering the execution of CT-Sim$_1$ and CT-Sim$_2$. This happens in an alternate manner, using time advance requests that trigger the execution of each CT simulator up to the next point in simulation time t_n. Each CT simulator returns an acknowledge message containing one of the following responses:

3.1. The completion of the execution up to time t_n.

3.2. The occurrence of a state event (refer to Definition 7.2) at a time $t_{se} < t_n$. In which case the CT simulator pauses its execution at t_{se}.

4. If a state event was detected, the coordinator must replace the next simulation time with the time of the state event $t_n = t_{se}$. The coordinator registers the new synchronization step to DE-Sim as a new timed event and adapts the simulation time of the CT simulators as follows:

4.1. If CT-Sim$_1$ was responsible for the state event, the execution of CT-Sim$_2$ will be instructed to execute up to the new t_n value.

4.2. If CT-Sim$_2$ was responsible for the state event, CT-Sim$_1$ must backtrack to the new t_n. Backtracking involves bringing the state of a simulator to a previous point in time. However, if the simulation engine of CT-Sim$_1$ does not support backtracking, then CT-Sim$_2$ should not be allowed to trigger state events. Similar considerations must be taken if further CT simulators with state event detection capabilities are used.

5. Once all CT simulators have reached t_n, DE-Sim is allowed to advance up to t_n, thus catching up in time with the rest of the simulators. Any number of delta-cycles may be executed by DE-Sim in which data synchronization with CT simulators is allowed. The simulation cycle returns to **STEP #2.** and is repeated until the simulation end has been reached or when the DE-Sim event queue becomes empty.

The transition diagram of Figure 7.8 shows the way in which simulators advance in a coupled DE/CT simulation. Specifically, it shows how the alternate execution of a DE simulator (DE-Sim) and two CT simulators (CT-Sim$_1$ and CT-Sim$_2$) can be coupled for enabling DE/CT co-simulation. The same principles apply for any number of CT simulators coupled to a DE simulator. The time points $(t_0, t_{n1}, t_{n2}, t_{n3}, ...)$ represent synchronization points that all simulators must reach in order to share information.

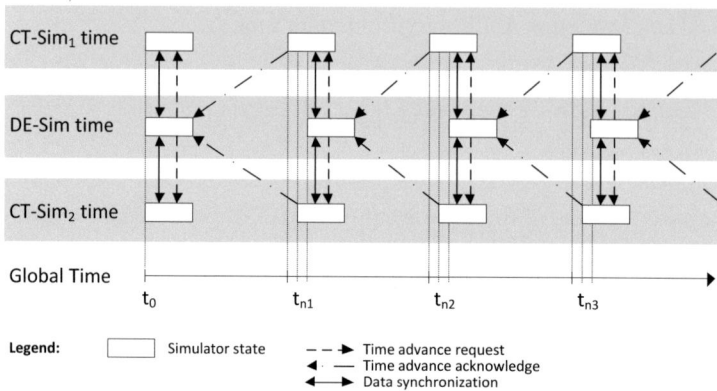

Figure 7.8: Transition diagram of DE/CT simulators

7.3.4 State event detection

State events are a useful mechanism to specify and detect discontinuities in AMS models. A common application is for modeling interrupt signals in AMS models which influence the execution of digital models. These interrupts are triggered whenever a continuous variable crosses a defined threshold. The time of the crossing must be first precisely detected and afterward added to the even queue of a DE-Sim in order to be processed at the exact simulation time in which it happened.

The effects of state events on the co-simulation cycle must be well understood in order to benefit from their advantages. This was already described in **STEP #4.** of the co-simulation cycle and will be further clarified with an example. Figure 7.9 is an excerpt from the transition diagram of Figure 7.8. For sake of simplicity, one DE-Sim and one CT-Sim are shown. In this example, the transition of a DE/CT co-simulation is as follows:

- Interval $[t_0, t_{n1}]$ *with no state events*:

  - ① DE-Sim initializes all its internal processes, afterward t_{n1} is selected. CT-Sim is given input data D_{DE} and requested to run up to t_{n1}.

  - ② CT-Sim simulates up to t_{n1} without any state event happening.

  - ③ CT-Sim acknowledges the time advance and gives DE-Sim input data D_{CT}.

  - ④ DE-Sim changes its current time to t_{n1} and executes the respective delta-cycles.

- Interval $[t_{n1}, t_{n2}]$ *with state events*:

    - ⑤ DE-Sim has finished executing all delta-cycles for t_{n1} and t_{n2} is selected. CT-Sim is given input data D_{DE} and requested to run up to t_{n2}.

    - ⑥ A state event at time $t_{se} < t_{n2}$ is detected by CT-Sim and stops at t_{se}.

    - ⑦ CT-Sim returns t_{se} and gives DE-Sim input data D_{CT}.

    - ⑧ DE-Sim changes its current time to t_{se} and executes the respective delta-cycles.

- Interval $[t_{se}, t_{n2}]$ *with no state events*:

    - ⑨ DE-Sim has finished executing all delta-cycles for t_{se} and a new t_{n2} is selected. CT-Sim is given input data D_{DE} and requested to run up to t_{n2}.

    - ⑩, ⑪, ⑫ are equivalent to steps ②, ③, ④.

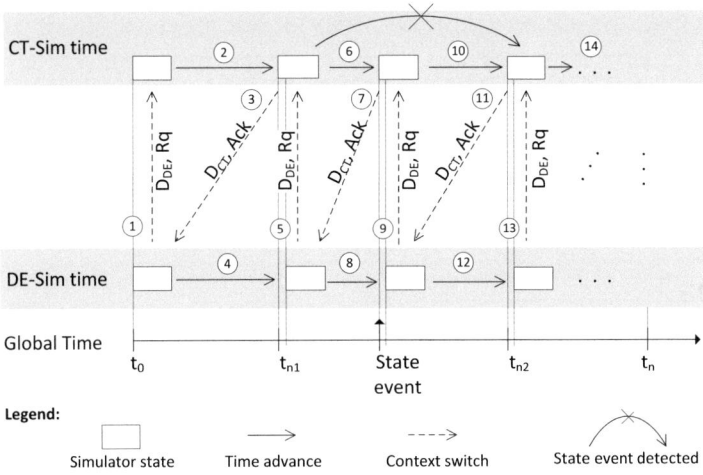

Figure 7.9: Exemplary transition diagram showing a state event detection

7.4 SystemC backplane

The open-source nature of the SystemC discrete-event (DE) simulator engine makes it a good candidate for DE/CT co-simulation. In this dissertation, SystemC is used as backplane for coupling DE and CT simulators as illustrated in Figure 7.10. Its simulation kernel is flexible enough to support the embedding of a coordinator inside an SC_MODULE and it is also flexible enough to be controlled by an external coordinator

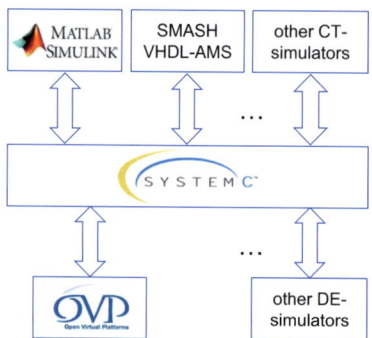

Figure 7.10: SystemC backplane

using available function calls. Therefore, this section presents a non-intrusive extension to the SystemC simulator that provides the required event introspection capabilities. This section also describes how the rest of the requirements for DE/CT co-simulation can be satisfied using available capabilities from the SystemC simulator. This knowledge will be later used in section Sections 7.5 and 7.6 for the co-simulation of SystemC with the CT simulators Simulink and Smash.

7.4.1 Event queue introspection

Event introspection capabilities are not supported by the latest SystemC version (v2.3.0). All data structures of a simulation are managed by the SystemC kernel simulation context class (`sc_simcontext`). The simulation context class is responsible for the execution of the simulation and contains references to all data structures, including event queues, used for this purpose. However, the access to this class is limited to kernel-level classes.

In order to enable event queue introspection capabilities, access to the simulation context from an external class is needed. This is achieved with a simple addition to the kernel, namely registering a `friend` class to the simulation context in order to look into its data structures. This addition is non-intrusive since the friend class is exclusively used to peek into the events queues of the simulation context without modifying them.

The sensitivity of a SystemC process is the set of events that can potentially cause the process to be resumed or triggered. Whenever an event is notified by its owner process, the event object itself is responsible for keeping a list of processes that are sensitive to it. Thus, when notified, the event object will inform the scheduler of which processes to trigger. Figure 7.11 shows how an event object interacts with its owner and the target processes it triggers. In the figure, it is also allowed for an owner and target process to

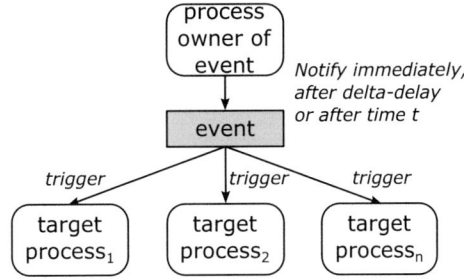

Figure 7.11: Event notification and process triggering

Event queue	Description
`m_methods_static`	Events notified after the `SC_METHOD` macro with the operator «
`m_methods_dynamic`	Events notified inside method processes with the function call `next_trigger`
`m_threads_static`	Events notified after the `SC_THREAD` macro with the operator «
`m_threads_dynamic`	Events notified inside thread processes with the function call `wait`

Table 7.1: Types of event queues in SystemC

be the same. This is the case for time event notifications such as `wait` (t), where the process yields until time t has elapsed.

Event objects that have been notified are classified and stored in the simulation context class into one of the four event queues shown in Table 7.1. Two of them are used for events notified from method processes (`SC_METHOD`) and two for events notified from thread processes (`SC_THREAD`). Each of these is used to store notified events for static or dynamic sensitivity. The difference between them is that static sensitivity is fixed during elaboration, while dynamic sensitivity may vary under the control of a process.

The modeling guidelines presented in Section 5.3 suggested the use of transaction level modeling abstraction for developing SystemC models. The reason behind this is that such models can be efficiently used for DE/CT co-simulation. Transaction level models are approximately-timed models where time annotations are done using `wait` function calls. Since `wait` calls are only allowed for thread processes [70], it can be inferred that the event queue that stores such timed events is `m_threads_dynamic`. Therefore, a DE/CT co-simulation coordinator must have access to `m_threads_dynamic`. Doing so enables the required event queue introspection for DE/CT co-simulation.

Obtaining detailed information of SystemC's event queues is not straightforward, even with full access to simulation context data structures. Montón's dissertation [99] provides useful insights on this topic. In his work, checkpointing capabilities for SystemC were investigated and for which the `m_methods_static` queue was required. Based on his work, Algorithm 1 was designed to access the `m_threads_dynamic` event queue and to obtain detailed information of the events inside it. The implementation of this algorithm must be compiled together with a SystemC model. Since it is only a method declared inside a C++ class, it can be called from a coordinator embedded in a SystemC module (Figure 7.6a) or external to SystemC (Figures 7.6b and 7.6c). It may also be called at any point of time during a simulation in order to obtain the event queue at that instant.

The event queue introspection algorithm works as follows. It initially obtains a list of all scheduled events (Line #2) where dynamically scheduled events (Line #4) are extracted from. The output is a vector called $EventQueueVec$ (Line #7) that contains the time of each event and the name of the SC_THREAD sensitive to it. The event queue vector can be afterward used by a DE/CT co-simulation coordinator, which can sort and filter it as required. The location of the coordinator (refer to Figure 7.6) does not affect the implementation of the event queue introspection algorithm since it only requires a pointer to the current simulation context.

Algorithm 1: Event queue introspection

Input: Pointer to the current simulation context $SimContext$
Output: Vector containing the event queue $EventQueueVec$

1 $TimeEventsList \leftarrow$ GetTimedEvents ($SimContext$) ;
   `// The list contains references to all dynamically and`
   `     statically scheduled events`
2 **forall the** $TimeEvent \in TimeEventList$ **do**
3      $time \leftarrow$ GetTime ($TimeEvent$);
       `// Find only dynamically scheduled events`
4      $SCthreadList \leftarrow$ GetDynThreads ($TimeEvent$);
       `// Multiple SC_THREADs may be sensitive to an event`
5   **forall the** $SCthread \in SCthreadList$ **do**
6          $target \leftarrow$ GetThreadName ($SCthread$);
7          $EventQueueVec \leftarrow (time, target)$;
8   **end**
9 **end**

7.4.2 Time advance detection

According to Section 7.3.2, the second requirement (-2.2.-) for a DE simulator to be used for DE/CT co-simulation is to provide means for detecting the last delta/cycle of a current time step. This is needed only when the coordinator is embedded into a SystemC module (Figure 7.6a). In this case, simulation starts with an `sc_start` call with no time arguments and runs until there is no more activity. Simulation time advances are automatically controlled by the SystemC scheduler, but they need to be somehow detected and controlled in order to synchronize data with CT simulators. In reference to Figure 7.7, this is needed at the end of ***STEP #5.*** of a DE/CT co-simulation, to detect when a DT simulator has finished executing all processes scheduled at time t_n. Detecting the last delta-cycle is important because it determines the point in simulation after which the SystemC scheduler advances simulation to the next scheduled time.

Time advance detection is possible in SystemC using available function calls in clever forms. There are two ways to do this. The first and simplest one is to use the publicly available SystemC function call `sc_pending_activity_at_current_time()`, which returns true if there are processes ready to run in the current time step. In order to use it for time advance detection, it must be declared inside an `SC_THREAD` which waits until there are no more processes pending, equivalent to the last delta-cycle of the current time step.

A second and more elegant way to detect time advances in SystemC is possible using SystemC's native trace mechanism. This technique relies on using a child class derived from SystemC trace class. Only one of the inherited methods is used, which will trigger a static callback function whenever the last delta-cycle of each time step has been reached. The callback function can be declared anywhere in a SystemC model, with the advantage that it does not have to be managed by the SystemC kernel as a thread. This approach was used by the time advance technique explained above. In this case, delta-cycles are automatically monitored using a native trace mechanism which has less overhead than using an `SC_THREAD`. Therefore, this approach is recommended for implementing time advance detection in SystemC.

7.4.3 Simulation control

The third and last requirement (-2.3.-) for a DE simulator to be used for DE/CT co-simulation is that it must be able to execute up to desired points in simulation time and resume execution afterward. This is only needed when an external coordinator is used to control the execution of SystemC (Figures 7.6b and 7.6c).

The typical way of executing a SystemC simulation is by calling the function `sc_start` inside the SystemC main function `sc_main`. When `sc_start` is called for the first time, the SystemC kernel performs an elaboration phase followed by a simulation phase. If an argument was passed to it, the scheduler will execute up to and including the latest delta-cycle of the end time. If no argument was passed, the scheduler will execute until there is no remaining activity. In addition, the SystemC standard [70] also allows `sc_start` calls with time arguments to be called multiple times. When this happens, the scheduler resumes from the time it had reached at the end of the previous call to `sc_start` and executes up to the current time plus the given time argument. Thus, the SystemC scheduler has the innate capability to be executed up to desired points in time and to resume its execution afterward. Moreover, calls to `sc_start` must not necessarily be done inside `sc_main`. In fact, `sc_start` can be called from any function compiled together with a SystemC model, even when such function is not registered with the SystemC kernel.

Therefore, an external coordinator is able to control the execution of a SystemC simulation by calling `sc_start` (with time arguments) as many times as required and from any function which is compiled together with a SystemC model. In addition, when using an external coordinator, the time advance detection capabilities described in Section 7.4.2 are not needed. Whenever an `sc_start` with a time argument is called, the SystemC scheduler will execute up to and including the last delta-cycle of the end time. In reference to Figure 7.7, this assures that the simulator is in **STEP #2.** of a DE/CT co-simulation and is ready to provide information about its event queue.

7.5 SystemC/Simulink co-simulation

This section presents the implementation of the DE/CT co-simulation scheme described in Section 7.3 for the coupling of the DE simulator SystemC and the CT simulator Simulink. In this particular implementation, the coordinator is embedded into Simulink (Figure 7.6b), which consequently makes Simulink the simulation master. The way in which SystemC and Simulink models are put together is by encapsulating a SystemC model, regardless of its complexity, as a Simulink actor. From a user point of view, a SystemC model is displayed in Simulink as a standard block with input and output ports. This actor is compatible with available Simulink models and libraries as long as a variable-step solver is used. The use of variable step solvers is actually very common. In fact, the *ode45* variable step solver is Simulink's default choice. The benefits of such co-simulation implementation is that users that are familiar with Simulink can seamlessly test SystemC models together with available models and libraries, while benefiting from the full simulation control and debugging capabilities offered by Simulink's intuitive and user friendly framework.

Related work on this topic [20, 21, 60, 104] uses SystemC as simulation master, which considerably decreases the acceptance of such approaches among Simulink users. The work presented in this section is derived from the author's publications [90, 91] and is the only work available at the moment that proposes using Simulink as simulation master for co-simulation with SystemC. Compared to the previous approaches, this approach increases simulation efficiency by providing improved ways for performing synchronization and increases its usability and acceptance among Simulink users. The integration of SystemC into Simulink is done in such a way that a user does not require any knowledge of the underlying SystemC model executing during the co-simulation.

7.5.1 Overview

Figure 7.12 shows the simulators and input files used for the implementation of System-C/Simulink co-simulation. Simulators for processor models, also known as instruction set simulators or processor emulators, can also be coupled to a virtual prototype (refer to Figure 5.4). In this case, the processor emulator tool OVP from Imperas was selected due to its compatibility with SystemC and its high simulation performance. Since the execution of processor model simulator is controlled solely by the SystemC scheduler, the DE/CT co-simulation scheme is not affected by it.

The virtual prototype shown in the middle of Figure 7.12 corresponds to a SystemC model of an embedded system. It is compiled as an executable or as a library and contains interfaces for communicating with the simulators around it. Once a virtual prototype is compiled, it does not necessarily mean that its structure is fixed. As with any other SystemC model, its structure is allowed to be modified as long as this is done before SystemC's elaboration phase is executed, after which the structure is completely defined and ready for simulation. More details on this topic can be found in the author's paper [90].

The configuration file shown in Figure 7.12 provides information for the parameterization of SystemC models and their interconnection with Simulink signals. It is imported and parsed on run-time, during the initialization phase of a SystemC model. A configuration file is divided in three sections: (1) parameters for the initialization of SystemC modules, (2) references for the interconnection of SystemC and Simulink signals and (3) verbose, logging, profiling and debugging options. The benefit of using

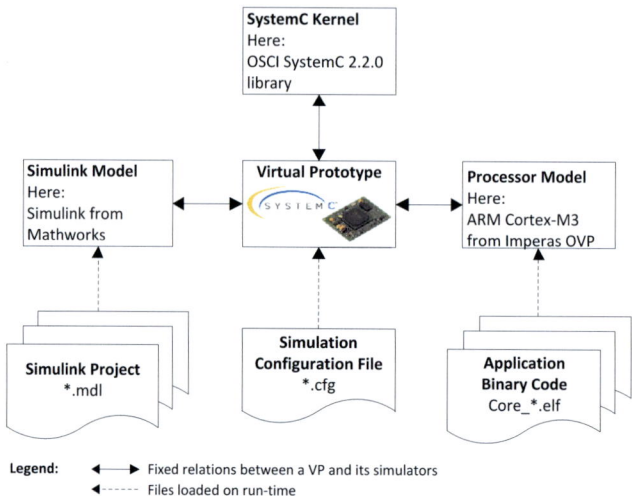

Figure 7.12: Tooling integration for SystemC/Simulink

a configuration file is that a SystemC model does not need to be recompiled each time parameters in a model are changed.

7.5.2 Implementation

Figure 7.13 shows the communication infrastructure that provides bidirectional data transfer capabilities between SystemC and Simulink. It is used for the initialization, parameterization and control of SystemC models from Simulink and for data synchronization during a co-simulation. The components of the communication infrastructure are explained ahead, starting from the bottom with the AMS channel.

AMS channel

An AMS channel is a C++ class that acts as a signal pool for storing references to SystemC and Simulink signals. Thus, all signals from SystemC and Simulink that need to communicate between each other must be connected to the AMS channel. The AMS channel is responsible for binding such signals and for performing subsequent data conversion that enables their compatibility. The data conversion involves the use of analog front end functions (refer to the AFE elements in Figure 5.4) which describe the quantization and de-quantization functions required for communicating digital signals from SystemC to conceptually analog signals from Simulink.

Middleware

A middleware defines the communication medium between an AMS channel from a SystemC model and an S-Function from Simulink. Only in the case where an AMS channel and an S-Function are compiled together, no external middleware is required. In such case, the communication is done by sharing pointers to a common memory space. However, when a AMS channel and an S-Function are executing in separate processes, inter-process communication (IPC) middleware such as TCP/IP or shared memory is required. The use of IPC middleware adds overhead to the communication, although it does not alter the co-simulation scheme. For sake of simplicity, this work assumes that the communication between an AMS channel and an S-Function is done in the same memory space and without the overhead of a middleware. Further details pertaining the evaluation of IPC middleware for the implementation of SystemC/Simulink co-simulation can be consulted in the author's paper [90].

S-Function

An S-function (system-function) is a computer language description of a Simulink block written in MATLAB, C, C++, or Fortran [129]. This work uses S-Functions developed in C++ for performing co-simulation with SystemC. Further details on the implementation of S-Functions for DE/CT co-simulation are presented in the following section.

Since an S-Function is developed in C++, it can be compiled together with a SystemC model, including its AMS-Channel. This explains why, in this case, the communication between them is done by passing references to addresses on the same memory space. Similarly, when using external middleware, the references being passed are either addresses to shared memory space [2] or CORBA-style function calls [37]. Therefore, the way in which communication is implemented between an S-Function and an AMS channel is independent of their functionality. A middleware is solely responsible for the communication.

7.5.3 Simulation configuration

According to Section 7.3.2, the first requirement (-1.-) for DE/CT co-simulation is that the simulators selected must be flexible enough to support the embedding of a coordinator or provide appropriate APIs to control them by an external coordinator. SystemC fulfills both conditions, although using SystemC as coordinator as shown in Figure 7.6a implies giving it simulation control instead of using Simulink's graphical interface for it. This reduces Simulink's usability, which consequently reduces the acceptance of

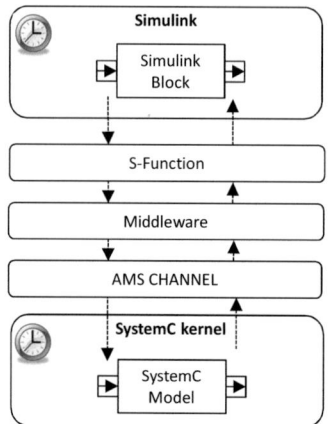

Figure 7.13: Communication infrastructure between SystemC and Simulink

the co-simulation among Simulink users. The second and most suitable option is to give Simulink simulation control. This is possible using S-Functions, which provide a powerful mechanism for extending the capabilities of Simulink. Thus, a coordinator can be embedded into an S-Function similarly to Figure 7.6b.

An S-Function consists of a series of interface methods that have access to Simulink's simulation engine data structures. S-Functions are used to describe the behavior of a user defined Simulink blocks. Its methods are compiled together as a dynamic library which is called by Simulink whenever its respective block is parameterized or executed during the course of a simulation. The scheduling of an S-Function during a simulation is responsibility of Simulink and is determined according to the type of sampling defined by the S-Function itself.

One S-Function is required for embedding the coordinator of a SystemC/Simulink co-simulation. The coordinator is responsible for carrying out the co-simulation scheme described in Section 7.3. Further capabilities are programed into the same S-Function which automates the following tasks: parameterization of SystemC models, binding of SystemC and Simulink signals, configuration of verbose, logging, profiling and debugging options.

The way in which all this functionality is fitted into an S-Function is described ahead. This will be done in reference to Figure 7.14, which shows the interface method calls used for this purpose. The Simulink simulation engine is responsible for the execution of such functions in the sequence defined in the figure. In order to describe them, they are initially classified into functions used for initialization and functions used for simulation.

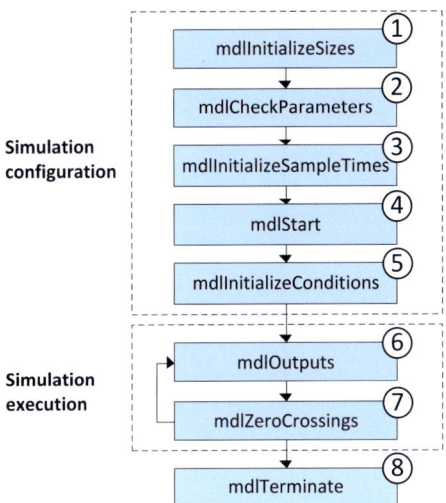

Figure 7.14: Structure of the S-Function co-simulation coordinator

Configuration manager

Functions `mdlInitializeSizes` and `mdlCheckParameters` from Figure 7.14 are used to gather configuration parameters for a virtual prototype and to create a configuration file accordingly. The configuration file contains the following information: (1) parameters for the initialization of SystemC modules inside a virtual prototype, (2) verbose, logging, profiling and debugging options and (3) references to Simulink signals that will be bound to SystemC signals. The created configuration file will be later on loaded and parsed by a SystemC virtual prototype in run-time as shown in Figure 7.12.

Data capture is done using an S-Function mask front-end. Figures 7.15a and 7.16 show examples of the configuration manager front-end. The different tabs in these examples correspond to parameterization and debugging information for different modules present in a SystemC model. This data is used to create the configuration file which is update whenever parameters change.

The I/O tab of the configuration manager makes it possible to reflect the I/O structure of a SystemC model into a Simulink block as shown in Figure 7.15. Thus, the number and type of I/O ports from a SystemC model are the same to those in its equivalent Simulink block. This one-to-one relation is done by binding the signals connected to each port of a Simulink block to their equivalent SystemC signal. Signal binding is responsibility of the AMS-Channel, which basically assigns pointers to Simulink signals to their SystemC signal counterparts.

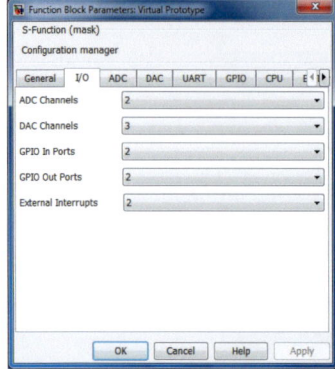

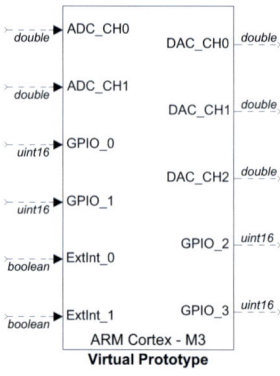

(a) Configuration manager - I/O   **(b)** Resulting Simulink block

Figure 7.15: Configuration of a virtual platform's I/O ports

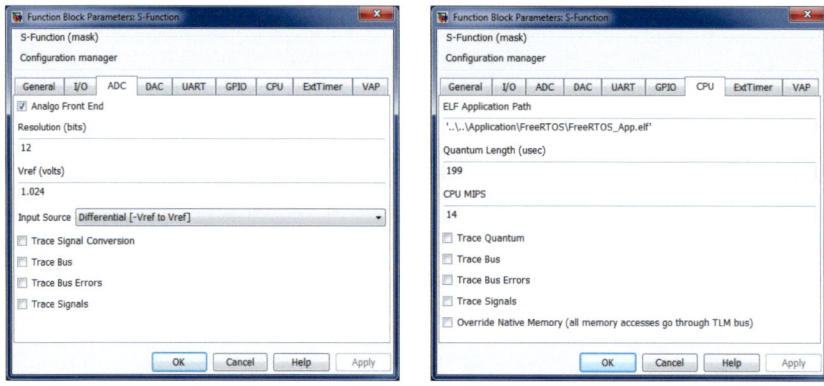

Figure 7.16: Configuration manager for ADC and CPU models

Sampling type settings

Function `mdlInitizlizeSampleTimes` from Figure 7.14 is used to define the sampling type of an S-Function. The sampling type chosen is crucial for a correct and efficient co-simulation with SystemC, since it determines when Simulink and SystemC are allowed to synchronize. There are three possibilities to do this, i.e. using discrete, variable or continuous sampling. A *discrete sampled* S-Function is called in fixed simulation steps and is an inefficient way to transfer data with SystemC's discrete event simulation kernel. A *variable sampled* S-Function is more efficient since its parameter "next-time-to-trigger" can be programed according to SystemC's event queue, avoiding unnecessary synchronization steps. However, a variable sampled S-Function is not adequate for co-simulation with SystemC since new synchronization points caused by the occurrence of state events (refer to Definition 7.2) cannot be reprogramed. The third possibility is to use *continuous sampling*, which is commonly used for physical models, but can be adapted for the co-simulation with SystemC as will be further explained. In continuous sampling, time advances in a series of major and minor time steps determined by an ODE solver according to a model's continuous states (Figure 7.5a) and/or according to the occurrence of state events (Figure 7.5b). The solver determines the times of the minor steps and uses the results at the minor time steps to improve the accuracy of the results at the major time steps.

According to Section 7.3.2, requirements -3.1.- and -3.2.- specify that the selected CT simulator must rely on a variable-step numerical integration solver and that it must provide zero-crossing detection mechanisms. Both conditions are fulfilled by a Simulink S-Function if and only if it is configured with continuous sampling. Since the S-Function does not have continuous states, it only needs to be updated in major time steps programed according to SystemC's event queue. This increases simulation performance since the S-Function does not need to be executed in minor time steps. State event detection is also possible using the S-Function's zero crossing detection mechanisms. Therefore, function mdlInitizlizeSampleTimes is configured as follows:

```
static void mdlInitializeSampleTimes(SimStruct *S){
    ssSetSampleTime(S, 0, CONTINUOUS_SAMPLE_TIME);
    ssSetOffsetTime(S, 0, FIXED_IN_MINOR_STEP_OFFSET);
}
```

7.5.4 Simulation execution

Initialization

The initialization of a SystemC virtual prototype is done inside function mdlStart. Algorithm 2 shows how this process is done and results in the first synchronization point for the co-simulation. This procedure corresponds to *STEP #1.* and *STEP #2.* of the DE/CT co-simulation cycle. Their implementation is described ahead.

After the instantiation of a virtual prototype, it is instructed to initialize by calling the function sc_start (*SC_ZERO_TIME*), which triggers SystemC's elaboration and initialization phases. The parameterization of a virtual prototype is performed automatically during SystemC's initialization phase, where the constructor of each SystemC module takes any parameter it requires from an available configuration file.

The event queue introspection mechanism described in Section 7.4.1 is executed afterward. It returns an event queue vector with two fields $(time, target)$, equivalent to the scheduled time of each event and the name of the target process it triggers. The vector is filtered according to the names of the SystemC processes that require synchronization with Simulink. The names of such processes are known beforehand, since they are specified in the configuration file. The earliest time from such list is assigned as the first point t_{n1} for performing synchronization.

Algorithm 2: S-Function `mdlStart` method

---

1   Instantiation of a SystemC virtual protype;
2   `sc_start (SC_ZERO_TIME)`;
3   $EventQueueVec \leftarrow$ `GetEventQueue` $(SimContext)$;
    `// Filter the event queue vector`
4   **forall the** $Event \in EventQueueVec$ **do**
5   $\quad$ **if** $Event[target] \in targetList$ **then**
6   $\quad\quad$ $tnList \leftarrow Event[time]$;
7   $\quad$ **end**
8   **end**
    `// Obtain the time of the first scheduled event`
9   $t_n \leftarrow$ `min` $(tnList)$;

The reason for performing filtering on SystemC's event queue is because not all timed events in it require data synchronization with Simulink. This increases simulation performance by reducing the amount of unnecessary synchronization points. For instance, the SystemC modules ADC, DAC, GPIO and Interrupt Controller may contain processes that require synchronization with Simulink since they perform I/O functionality. The name of such processes as well as any other processes that requires I/O functionality must be added to the event filter list.

Time advance control

In a continuous sampled S-Function, time advances are determined by an ODE solver according to the rate of change of the continuous states of a model and/or according to nonsampled zero crossings. In this case, since the S-Function does not contain any continuous states, it implies that time advances can only be done according to nonsampled zero crossings. This means there is no fixed or variable sampling times. The question is then, how to indicate to the Simulink engine that the S-Function must be sampled at times equal to SystemC's next time event t_n?

The first insights to this question are given by TrueTime [29], a Simulink library for networked embedded control systems developed at Lund University. In TrueTime, a kernel similar to an RTOS is used to schedule tasks designed to control Simulink models. The sampling type chosen for TrueTime is also continuous, even though its kernel has no continuous states. A similar question as stated above arises when trying to schedule tasks from the TrueTime kernel based on Simulink's simulation engine time. The solution used by TrueTime is based on an S-Function's zero crossing mechanism, which is programed to automatically trigger a notification each time the Simulink's time reaches the time schedule for a TrueTime kernel task.

Similarly to TrueTime, an S-Functions's zero crossing mechanisms are harnessed for the co-simulation between Simulink and SystemC. A zero crossing function is used to detect when Simulink's engine time has reached SystemC's next time event ($t_{Simulink} = t_n$). A notification is triggered afterward which is used to perform synchronization between Simulink and SystemC.

Algorithm 3 shows the implementation of the zero crossing function using the S-Function method `mdlZeroCrossings`. The algorithm is used to lock Simulink's engine time $t_{Simulink}$ to SystemC's next time event t_n. Whenever $t_{Simulink}$ goes over t_n, a zero crossing is forced by changing the sign of a threshold signal. Simulink simulation engine is responsible for finding the exact time of the crossing using a bisection algorithm. Once a zero crossing has been triggered, Simulink engine calls Algorithm 3 until the zero crossing is detected with a specified accuracy or the maximum number of zero crossing iterations is reached. Both accuracy and the number of iterations are parameters of any Simulink variable step solver and can be adapted if necessary.

Algorithm 3: S-Function `mdlZeroCrossings` method

---

1 **if** $t_{Simulink} < t_n$ **then**
2 　| 　$ZCThreshold \leftarrow -1$;
3 **end**
4 **else if** $t_{Simulink} > t_n$ **then**
5 　| 　$ZCThreshold \leftarrow +1$;
6 **end**
7 **else**
8 　| 　$ZCThreshold \leftarrow 0$;
9 **end**

State event detection

The most obvious application of state event detection in model-based design of embedded systems is for modeling the behavior of interrupt detection mechanisms. In the case of Simulink/SystemC co-simulation, interrupt signals are generated in Simulink while their Interrupt Service Routines are declared inside a SystemC model. This requires for Simulink to notify SystemC of the exact time of the occurrence of an event on an interrupt signal.

As described in the previous section, state event detection is an innate capability of a continuous sampled S-Function. Before the start of a simulation, the configuration manager automatically registers all input ports of type `bool` with zero crossing capabilities. Events on these ports are monitored by the Simulink engine during simulation. Whenever an event occurs, the simulation engine detects the time of the occurrence and executes the S-Function method `mdlOutputs`. This is done automatically by Simulink, without specifying any additional zero crossing functions. This corresponds to *STEP #3.* of the DE/CT co-simulation cycle.

Simulation cycle

The S-Function method `mdlOutputs` is used to implement *STEP #4.*, *STEP #5.* and the loop back to *STEP #2.* of the DE/CT co-simulation cycle (refer to Figure 7.7). Algorithm 4 shows how this is implemented.

Since the S-Function has no continuous states, the method `mdlOutputs` is executed only when nonsampled zero crossings are detected. There are two possible sources for this: first, when Simulink time has reached a programed SystemC next time event and second, due to the occurrence of a state event on an interrupt port. These two situations will be explained ahead.

The first case corresponds to *STEP #5.* of the DE/CT co-simulation cycle. It happens when the condition $t_n \leq t_{Simulink}$ is met (Line #1), meaning that Simulink has reached SystemC's next time event. SystemC is lagging in time, so it must be executed up to t_n to catch up with Simulink (Line #3). During its execution, SystemC is allowed to perform I/O operation on any Simulink signal connected to it, which is coherent since both simulators share the same time. *STEP #2.* of the DE/CT co-simulation cycle follows since a new t_n must be obtained from SystemC's even queue. SystemC event queue is obtained using the introspection mechanism described in Section 7.4.1. The event queue vector is then filtered according to the names of the SystemC processes that require synchronization with Simulink and the earliest time from the resulting list is selected as t_n (Line #10). This new t_n value is used by Algorithm 3 for triggering a new zero crossing.

The second case corresponds to *STEP #4.* of the DE/CT co-simulation cycle. It is the result of the occurrence of a state event on an interrupt port (Line #12). All interrupt ports must be scanned to find out the port where the state event happened. This is done by comparing the current state of each port with stored values corresponding to their previous state. Once the interrupt port responsible for the state event is detected, SystemC time must catch up with the time of the state event (Line #15). During its execution, SystemC will trigger the execution of the corresponding Interrupt Service Routine at the exact simulation time in which it happened. The execution might have affected SystemC's event queue, thus a new t_n must be obtained using the same procedure as before, i.e. looking into the event queue, filtering it and obtaining the earliest time from it. This new t_n value is used by Algorithm 3 for triggering a new zero crossing.

Simulation termination

Simulation termination is implemented in the S-Function method `mdlTerminate`. It is called when the specified simulation time has elapsed or when SystemC event queue has no time events in its event queue. The termination method destroys the instance to the SystemC virtual prototype and frees all data structures used for such purpose. This makes it possible to rerun a co-simulation as many times as required.

Algorithm 4: S-Function `mdlOutputs` method

    // Check if Simulink time has reached t_n
1 **if** $t_n \leq t_{Simulink}$ **then**
2      $t_{diff} \leftarrow (t_n - t_{SystemC})$
       // Catch up SystemC with Simulink time
3   sc_start (t_{diff});
4      $EventQueueVec \leftarrow$ GetEventQueue $(SimContext)$;
       // Filter the event queue vector
5   **forall the** $Event \in EventQueueVec$ **do**
6   **if** $Event[target] \in targetList$ **then**
7            $tnList \leftarrow Event[time]$;
8   **end**
9   **end**
       // Obtain the time of the next scheduled event
10     $t_n \leftarrow$ min $(tnList)$;
11 **end**
    // Check for the occurrence of state events
12 **forall the** $Ports \in InterruptPorts$ **do**
       // Locate the interrupt port where the state event
       happened
13   **if** $Port[PrevState] \neq Port[CurrState]$ **then**
14        $t_{diff} \leftarrow (t_{Simulink} - t_{SystemC})$
          // Catch up SystemC to the time of the state event
15   sc_start (t_{diff});
16        $EventQueueVec \leftarrow$ GetEventQueue $(SimContext)$;
          // Filter the event queue vector
17   **forall the** $Event \in EventQueueVec$ **do**
18   **if** $Event[target] \in targetList$ **then**
19              $tnList \leftarrow Event[time]$;
20   **end**
21   **end**
          // Obtain the time of the first scheduled event
22        $t_n \leftarrow$ min $(tnList)$;
23   **end**
24 **end**

7.6 SystemC/VHDL-AMS co-simulation

This section presents the implementation of the DE/CT co-simulation scheme described in Section 7.3 for the coupling of the DE simulator SystemC and the CT simulator Smash for VHDL-AMS models. In this particular implementation, the coordinator is embedded into SystemC (Figure 7.6a), which consequently makes SystemC the simulation master. From a user point of view, this means that the co-simulation starts by executing a SystemC virtual prototype.

In comparison to the SystemC/Simulink approach described above, the DE/CT co-simulation principles are the same, but their implementation varies considerably. The reason is the location of the coordinator, which in this case is embedded into SystemC.

7.6.1 Overview

Figure 7.17 shows the simulators and input files used for the implementation of System-C/VHDL-AMS co-simulation. It is also possible to couple a processor model simulator used for the execution of PE_3 models (refer to Figure 5.4). The SystemC virtual prototype in the middle of the figure is compiled as an executable application responsible for initializing and controlling the simulators around it.

A configuration file, loaded on run-time in the initialization phase, contains the necessary information for the virtual platform to locate the paths to the VHDL-AMS project and the binary application code for the processor model. Additionally, the configuration file contains all the necessary initialization and debugging parameters to configure each component of the virtual platform. The extension of the configuration file depends on the complexity of the model. It enables full testing and debugging flexibility without the need to recompile or create new versions of the virtual platform. Further details on this topic are presented in Section 7.6.3.

7.6.2 Implementation

Figure 7.18 shows the communication infrastructure used to provide bidirectional data transfer capabilities between SystemC and Smash. The components of the communication infrastructure are explained ahead, starting from the bottom with the AMS channel.

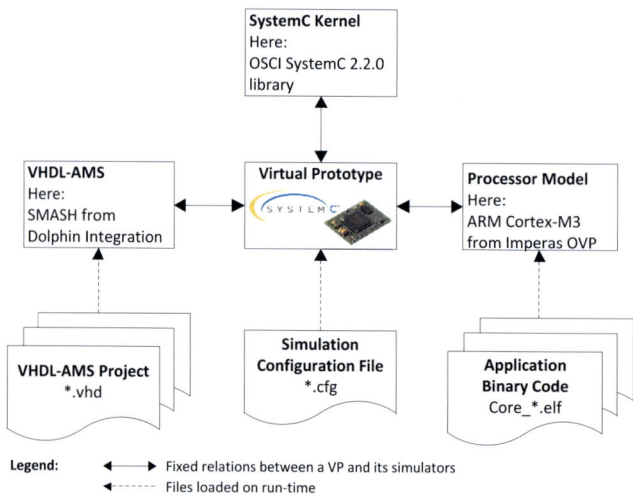

Figure 7.17: Tooling integration for SystemC/VHDL-AMS

AMS channel

An AMS channel is a C++ class that acts as a signal pool for storing references to SystemC and VHDL-AMS signals. Thus, all signals from SystemC and VHDL-AMS that need to communicate between each other must be connected to the AMS channel. The AMS channel is responsible for binding such signals and for performing subsequent data conversion that enables their compatibility. The data conversion involves the use of analog front end functions (refer to the AFE elements in Figure 5.4) which describe the quantization and de-quantization functions required for communicating digital signals from SystemC to conceptually analog signals from VHDL-AMS.

APIs

Smash provides multiple API functions in the form of dynamic link libraries (DLL). They are intended to extend the functionalities of Smash by providing specialized functions for controlling and tweaking various aspects of a simulation. These APIs can also be used to control Smash from an external application, namely from the AMS channel of a SystemC model.

According to Section 7.3.2, the first requirement (-1.-) for DE/CT co-simulation is that the simulators selected must be flexible enough to support the embedding of a coordinator or provide appropriate APIs to control them by an external coordinator. Smash fulfills the second condition since it provides multiple APIs for its control from

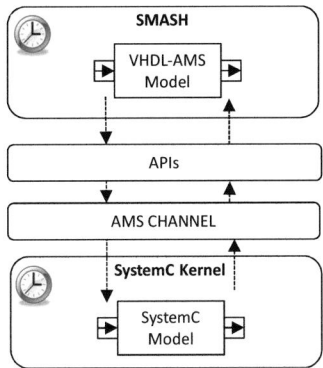

Figure 7.18: Communication infrastructure between SystemC and Smash

an external coordinator, namely SystemC. This is done by compiling references to such APIs together with the AMS channel of a Simulink model. Therefore, it is possible from a SystemC model to load any VHDL-AMS model into Smash and control every detail of its execution in Smash.

7.6.3 Simulation configuration

A configuration file such as the one shown in Figure 7.19 is used to configure the SystemC/VHDL-AMS co-simulation. This file is equivalent to the one created with the help of an S-Function mask in the SystemC/Simulink implementation. However, since neither SystemC nor Smash provide a suitable graphical interface for specifying such options, they must be manually configured inside a file.

The configuration file contains the following information : (1) parameters for the initialization of SystemC modules inside a the virtual prototype, (2) verbose, logging, profiling and debugging options and (3) references to VHDL-AMS signals that will be bound to SystemC signals. The configuration file will be later on loaded and parsed by a SystemC virtual prototype in run-time as shown in Figure 7.17.

7.6.4 Simulation execution

The difference between the SystemC/VHDL-AMS co-simulation implementation and its SystemC/Simulink counterpart from the previous section relies on the location of the coordinator. In this case, the coordinator executes inside the AMS-Channel of a SystemC model.

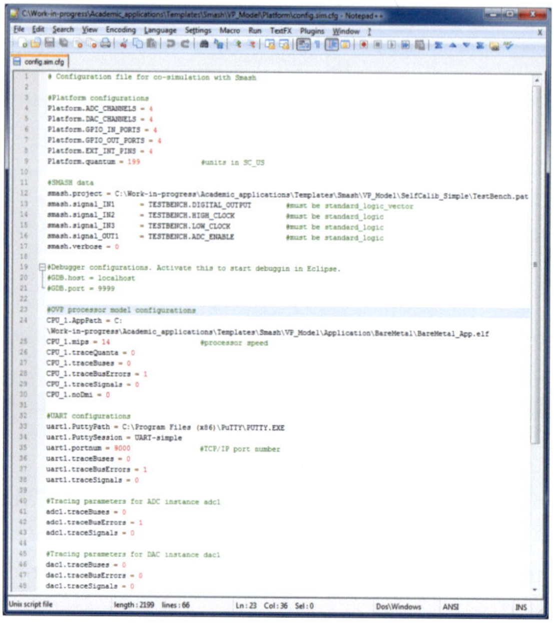

Figure 7.19: Example of a configuration file for SystemC/VHDL-AMS co-simulation

A key factor for any co-simulation where SystemC acts as simulation master is the detection of SystemC time advances. In contrast, when SystemC acts as simulation slave, there is no need to identify time advances since they are already implied by the `sc_start` function calls triggered by an external simulator. In this case, the function `sc_start` is called once and runs until the completion of the simulation. A solution for the automatic detection of SystemC time advances was described in Section 7.4.2. This mechanism automatically triggers a callback function called `TimeAdvance` after the end of each delta cycle, just before the SystemC kernel advances time (refer to Definition 7.2). The function `TimeAdvance` is implemented as a method belonging to the AMS channel.

Initialization

No special initialization sequence is required since the call to `sc_start` automatically elaborates the SystemC model and initializes all processes in it. The first call to `TimeAdvance` is automatically triggered after SystemC's initialization phase. This corresponds to *STEP #1.* of the DE/CT co-simulation cycle.

State event detection

The most obvious application of state event detection in model-based design of embedded systems is for modeling the behavior of interrupt detection mechanisms. In the case of SystemC/VHDL-AMS co-simulation, interrupt signals are generated using VHDL-AMS quantity signals while their Interrupt Service Routines are declared inside a SystemC model. This requires for Smash to notify SystemC of the exact time of the occurrence of an event on an interrupt signal.

This is done by assigning *break* statements to VHDL-AMS quantity signals that trigger interrupt ports in a SystemC model. Such *break* statements are executed whenever a given threshold is crossed. The exact time in which a break statement is executed is automatically detected by the Smash simulation engine using a backtrack mechanism that locks to the time of the occurrence. The way in which such state event times are used for the co-simulation with SystemC is described ahead.

Simulation cycle

The simulation cycle is executed inside the function `TimeAdvance`, which acts as coordinator for the co-simulation. The procedure followed by the simulation cycle is described in Algorithm 5 and corresponds to the following steps of the DE/CT co-simulation cycle:

DE/CT co-simulation stage from Figure 7.7	Relation to Algorithm 5
STEP #2.	Line #1 to 7
STEP #3.	Line #8 to 28
STEP #4.	Line #17 to 24

Time advances during the simulation cycle are determined according to SystemC timed events. The time of these events determine how simulation time is advanced. They are obtained by looking into SystemC's event queue with the event introspection mechanism described in Section 7.4.1. The event queue is afterwards filtered according to timed event that require synchronization with VHDL-AMS. This is possible since the name of all SystemC processes which require I/O functionality with VHDL-AMS are listed in the configuration file. Thus, only timed events targeting processes listed in the configuration file are filtered. The earliest time from the resulting list is selected as t_n (Line #7). This t_n value is used to advance the simulation of the VHDL-AMS simulator.

The simulation of a VHDL-AMS model requires an analog simulator for the AMS part of the model and a logical simulator for the digital part of the model [69]. Smash

---

Algorithm 5: SystemC/VHDL-AMS simulation control

---

1   $EventQueueVec \leftarrow$ GetEventQueue $(SimContext)$;
    // Filter the event queue vector
2   **forall the** $Event \in EventQueueVec$ **do**
3   **if** $Event[target] \in targetList$ **then**
4           $tnList \leftarrow Event[time]$;
5   **end**
6   **end**
    // Obtain the time of next scheduled event
7   $t_n \leftarrow \min(tnList)$;
    // Execute transient sequence of VHDL-AMS simulator
8   $timeStep \leftarrow$ initial time step size;
9   **while** $timeStep \leq t_n$ **do**
10   **repeat**
11   SolveAnalog $(timeStep)$;
12   **if** $!AnalgoConvergence$ **then**
13          $timeStep \leftarrow$ adjust $timeStep$;
14   **end**
15   **until** $AnalogConvergence$;
16   SolveLogic $(timeStep)$;
17   **if** $stateEvent$ **then**
        // Backtrack VHDL-AMS simulator
18       $timeStep \leftarrow t_{se}$;
19       $t_n \leftarrow t_{se}$;
20   **forall the** $Ports \in InterruptPorts$ **do**
          // Locate the interrupt port where the state
             event happened and trigger an event on it
21   **if** $Port[PrevState] \neq Port[CurrState]$ **then**
22             $Port \leftarrow$ NotifySystemCEvent (t_{se});
23   **end**
24   **end**
25   **else**
26       $timeStep \leftarrow$ calculate next $timeStep$;
27   **end**
28   **end**

VHDL-AMS simulator provides APIs for controlling both analog and logical simulators. Thus, it is possible from SystemC to control every detail for the simulation of VHDL-AMS models. This capability is exploited for the detection of state events and their notification to SystemC. Whenever a state event is detected during the simulation of a VHDL-AMS model, the time of the state event and the port in which it happened are notified to SystemC using a timed event notification (Line #22). This triggers an Interrupt Service Routine on the port and time specified next time SystemC is executed.

After the execution of Algorithm 5, the method `TimeAdvance` finishes and yields control back to the SystemC scheduler. The SystemC scheduler advances the sate of the simulation to the next timed event t_n. This corresponds to **STEP #5.** of the DE/CT co-simulation cycle. Only when a state event was detected during the execution of a VHDL-AMS model, the next time in the event queue corresponds to time t_{se}. `TimeAdvance` will be automatically triggered when all delta cycles for the new time step have finished, thus repeating the simulation cycle.

Simulation termination

Simulation termination is determined by the SystemC scheduler. This happens when the specified simulation time has elapsed or when the event queue has no more timed events in it. All references to Smash VHDL-AMS simulator are afterwards destroyed. This makes it possible to rerun a co-simulation as many times as required.

8

Evaluation

This chapter presents an evaluation of the multi-domain virtual prototyping design and verification methodology described in the previous chapters. Two recent implementation examples are considered: an academic case study that was published in [91] and an industrial case study that was published in [92]. The first describes the design and verification of a PID close-loop control system. The second describes the verification of a novel Rogowski Current Coil Transducer (RCCT) electronic front end architecture and its online auto-calibration software algorithm.

8.1 PID close-loop control system

The proposed methods and tools described in this dissertation where applied for the design and verification of a digital PID controller for a temperature-control system described in [109]. Three SystemC based digital controllers were created following the abstraction layers presented in Section 6.1. They were made available as components of a Simulink library and used in the test setup from Figure 8.1 to verify the behavior of their PID algorithm implementations for controlling the temperature of a physical model described in Simulink.

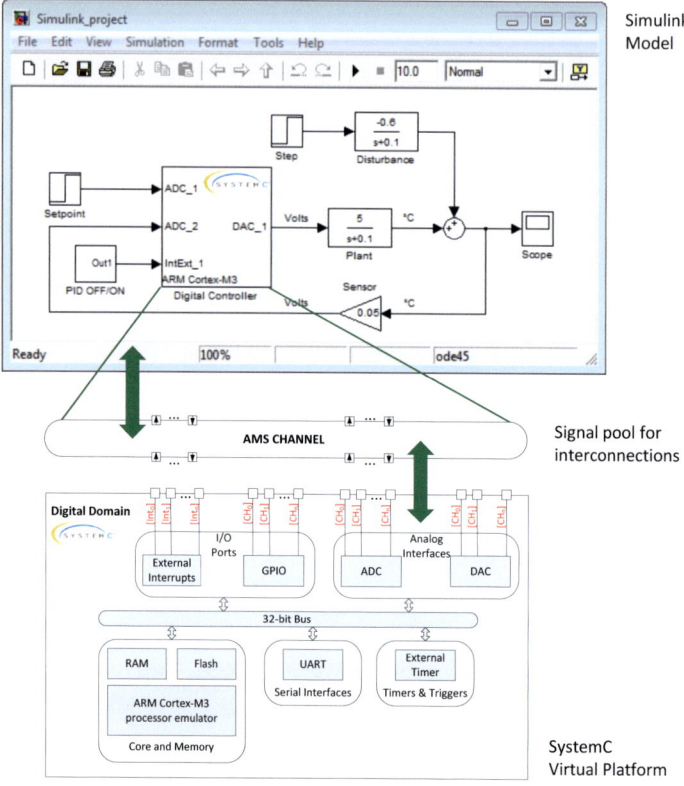

Figure 8.1: Implementation-oriented virtual prototype for a temperature-control system

8.1.1 Simulation models

The design and verification procedure of a digital PID controller algorithm using available concept-oriented, architecture-oriented and implementation-oriented virtual prototypes will be further explained. The PID algorithm was manually coded C-based implementation.

In the concept-oriented virtual prototype from Figure 8.2a, the PID algorithm is inserted in the SW Stack as a task with direct access to I/O ports for data transfer with Simulink. Additionally, the SW Stack includes one ISR sensitive to an external interrupt that toggles the activation of the PID task. Time advances in the model via a *wait(100,SC_MS)* statement in the PID task.

In the architecture-oriented virtual prototype from Figure 8.2b, the PID algorithm is inserted in the SW Stack as a task with access to peripheral SW drivers. The ADC is configured to sample input data from Simulink on a 100*msec* rate with 16-bit resolution.

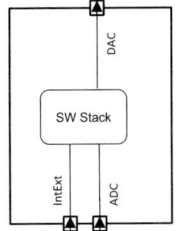

(a) Concept-Oriented VP

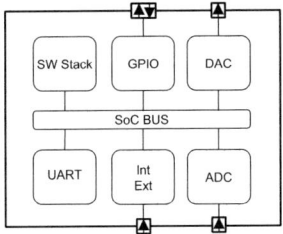

(b) Architecture-Oriented VP

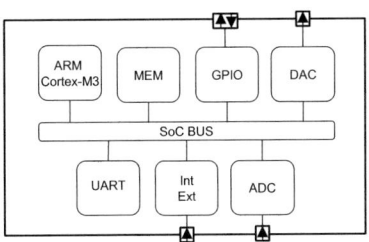

(c) Implementation-Oriented VP

Figure 8.2: Subsequent refinements of a virtual prototype

ISRs for the ADC and one external interrupt are added. The PID task activation is controlled by a semaphore trigged by the ADC ISR, at which point the computations from the PID algorithm are executed and data is sent to Simulink via DAC SW drivers.

The implementation-oriented virtual prototype from Figure 8.2c contains an ARM Cortex-M3 processor emulator (OVP processor model from Imperas [73]). The SW Stack contains a ported distribution of FreeRTOS. The PID algorithm, ADC configuration and ISRs for ADC and external interrupts are included to the SW Stack in a similar procedure to the architecture-oriented virtual prototype. The main difference is that SystemC specific constructs are replaced by FreeRTOS constructs. The complete SW Stack is cross-complied and loaded to a memory peripheral, where it is fetched by the ARM Cortex-M3 model on run-time.

8.1.2 Simulation results

Figure 8.3 shows the simulation results for each of the three SystemC based virtual prototypes controlling the temperature of the Simulink physical plant models from Figure 8.1. For comparison purposes, the simulation results from a reference model developed in Simulink with a PID block from the discrete time toolbox are also shown. All simulations were done using a standard desktop PC. Table 8.1 shows the simulation times for each model.

Figure 8.4 presents the relative temperature differences of the physical plant models controlled by the SystemC based virtual prototypes. The results are presented with respect to a Simulink reference model. The manually coded PID algorithm implementation is different to the one used by Simulink's PID block. This becomes evident when the PID models initialize (100-125% peeks between 1-1.1sec that are not shown in the graph) and when they are reseted. An anti-windup PID algorithm implementation could be used to solve this issue. It is also interesting to see that relative differences are bigger for the implementation-oriented virtual prototype, which computes the same PID algorithm implementation, however complied with another compiler for a different processor architecture.

8.1.3 Evaluation

This simple application demonstrates the feasibility of coupling different domain specific models and their simulators for the creation of virtual prototypes. These virtual prototypes provide debugging and tracing capabilities that can help improve the understanding of the composite behavior of a system during different stage of the design. The obtained simulation performance is acceptable and slow-downs are mainly caused by the increase of granularity in models.

This example demonstrates that once the required models to build a virtual platform are available, their implementation in the design and verification of heterogeneous embedded systems for domain-specific applications is viable. As with any new model-

Model name	Simulation time
Simulink reference model	0.65 sec
Concept-oriented VP	0.89 sec
Architecture-oriented VP	2.37 sec
Implementation-oriented VP	11.82 sec

Table 8.1: Execution times for different simulation models

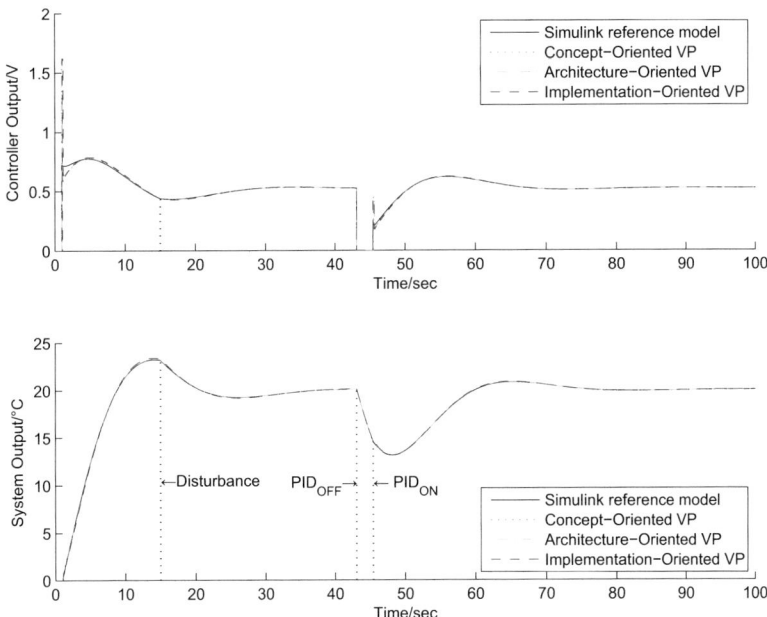

Figure 8.3: Simulation results of the three SystemC based virtual prototypes and a Simulink reference model

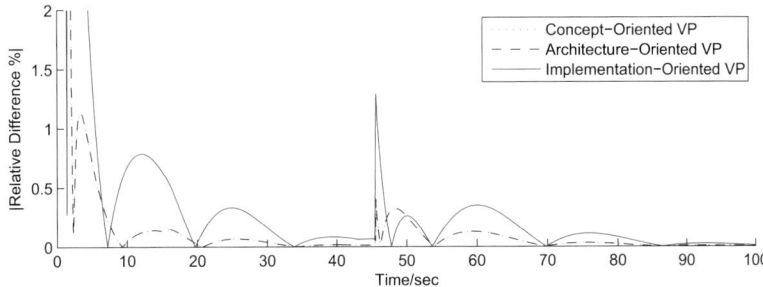

Figure 8.4: Relative output temperature differences with respect to a Simulink reference model

based design approach, its implementation effort is initially high, but as more components are added to a library and reused in other projects, the effort will evidently decrease.

8.2 Rogowski Coil Current Transducer

Rogowski Coil Current Transducers (RCCT) are used in medium voltage industrial and power distribution systems for current measurement applications. In [107], a new electronic front end architecture for a RCCT was presented that enables online self-calibration. It is a novel design that allows higher accuracy than conventional solutions and at a lower cost.

8.2.1 Operation principle

A short explanation of the new RCCT read out electronics architecture and its online calibration functionality are given ahead, for more details refer to [107]. Figure 8.5 shows a simplified schematic of the RCCT and its electronic front end. The distinctive characteristic of this architecture is the use of a modulation circuit inserted between nodes P and S. It uses a square signal carrier of known amplitude V_{ref} and controllable frequency to modulate the input voltage V_S. The modulated signals are then fed to the summing points S of the amplifier and to an ADC. Throughout this process, the resulting signal will inevitably suffer unwanted drifts due to aging and temperature effects on the amplifier high impedance resistors $R_{1,3}$ and on the ADC conversion gain, affecting the overall accuracy of the current measurement. A digital system (not shown in the figure) is responsible for demodulating the ADC readings, in which process it detects unwanted drifts introduced by the electronic front end. Samples are corrected on run-time without interrupting the measurement by removing the previously calculated drift. This procedure results in highly accurate current measurement results.

8.2.2 Simulation models

The reason for performing simulations of the RCCT, its analog front end architecture and its embedded controller software algorithm was to verify its overall functionality and to perform a feasibility study of possible digital and AMS hardware implementation solutions. The first is possible because all models can be simulated and are able to interact with each other in a correct and predictable way. The latter is also possible because a processor model is used that emulates the instruction set of an available microcontroller. In addition, AMS models are constructed based on physical models of real hardware

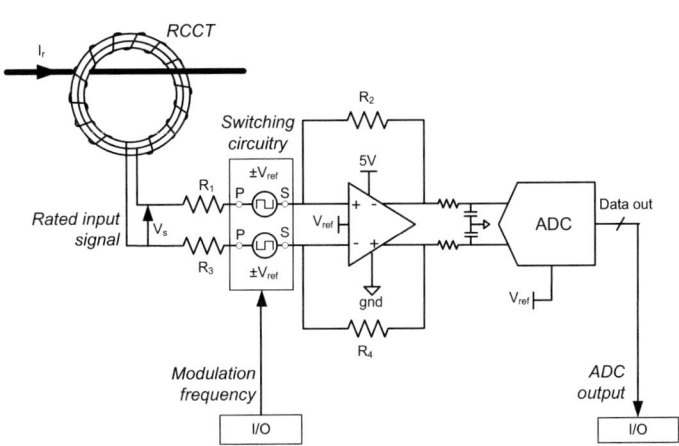

Figure 8.5: Simplified schematic of the new online self-calibration architecture applied to a RCCT read out electronic front end [107]. The transducer output voltage V_S is proportional to the derivate of the current and must be integrated. The integration is done digitally in a later stage.

implementations. The validity of the results is therefore based on the correctness of our models, so a considerable amount of effort was invested in verifying each component. The advantage is that such components can be later on reused and refined in other projects with a considerably lower modeling and verification effort.

The overall system was modeled by different project team-members, each one specializing in a particular aspect of the design and using different domain specific languages and tools. VHDL-AMS was used for modeling the RCCT and the electronic front end. The VHDL-AMS simulator chosen was SMASH from Dolphin Integration. SystemC was used for modeling a virtual platform using, among other digital components, an ARM Cortex-M3 processor model from Imperas OVP tools. Embedded software was developed in an Eclipse IDE framework using a GCC based ARM EABI cross-compiler and linker.

The resulting virtual platform contains the following components (refer to the metastructure from Figure 5.4): one PE_3 element (controls OVP API functions), one 32-bit SoC memory mapped bus, several peripherals and their AFE counterparts and one AMS Channel (controls SMASH API functions). A configuration file, loaded on run-time in an initialization phase, contains the necessary information for the virtual platform to locate the paths to the VHDL-AMS project and the binary application code for the processor model. Additionally, the configuration file contains all the necessary initialization and debugging parameters to configure each component of the virtual platform. The extension of the configuration file depends on the complexity of the model. It enables full testing and debugging flexibility without the need to recompile or create new versions of the virtual platform.

Figure 8.6 shows a system level view of the virtual platform, the models involved and how they are related with each other. VHDL-AMS signals of type *electrical* must be converted to their digital equivalent before being handled by a digital model. This is done by a simplified 16-bit ADC model with a 4kHz output rate. VHDL-AMS digital signals of type *STD_LOGIC* and *STD_LOGIC_VECTOR* are allowed to connect to the AMS Channel where signals from SystemC AFE models are also connected. The binding between them is specified inside the configuration file in a text-based format as follows:

```
AMS_CH.ADC_CH0 = SMASH.DIGITAL_OUTPUT
AMS_CH.GPIO_0  = SMASH.ADC_ENABLE
AMS_CH.GPIO_1  = SMASH.HIGH_CLOCK
AMS_CH.GPIO_2  = SMASH.LOW_CLOCK
```

8.2.3 Simulation results

A data logger module, shown in Figure 8.6, was added to the virtual platform to store 32-bit length packages generated by the processor. Since it is connected to the SoC bus, it can be accessed by the embedded software via SW drivers as any other peripheral. Its advantage is that it requires a considerably lower processor load than a serial interface communication.

The overall functionality of the system was verified manually based on signal traces stored by the logger module. The simulation performance is equivalent to real-time, thus test runs can be rapidly carried out. VHDL-AMS models and the embedded code can be rapidly modified and tested together with the rest of the virtual platform.

Figure 8.7 shows the measurement data received by the processor. It corresponds to the electronic front end ADC output. We clearly see that the measured signal contains two kinds of information: the RCCT rated sinusoidal signal at 50Hz and the square modulated reference signal at 2.5Hz. These two signals have been superimposed by the electronic front end. The embedded software algorithm inside the processor synchronously demodulates the ADC output data, detects the drift and corrects it on run-time. The corrected signal is displayed in the lower graph of Figure 8.7.

The corrected signal presents transient errors caused by the $\pm V_{ref}$ transition of the 2.5Hz modulated reference. The reason behind them will be further explained. In each

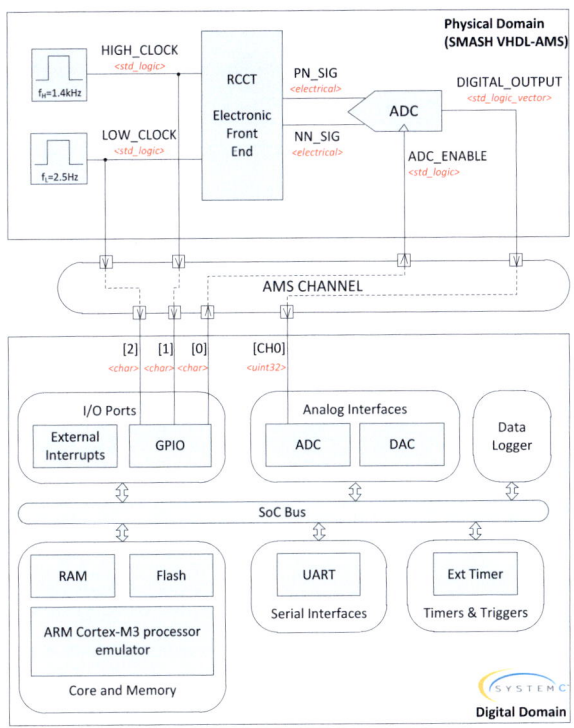

Figure 8.6: System level model of the virtual platform. The RCCT electronic front end and its embedded controller are shown.

$\pm V_{ref}$ transition point, the ADC receives a step function input whose response needs a certain time, also called group delay, to propagate through a series of digital filters. During such time intervals, the correction algorithm receives unsettled input samples from the ADC which cannot be compensated by the correction algorithm, thus creating erroneous results seen as spikes in the output signal. Even though the step response of the ADC is deterministic and its effects could be compensated in software, its response in combination with an amplifier and anti-aliasing filter is not fully deterministic. The step response of the ADC will slightly vary in each hardware implementation due to tolerances, ageing and temperature dependencies of analog components from the electronic front end. From our simulation models, we were able to determine that remaining spikes in the corrected signal will not interfere the measurement results if their frequency components do not superimpose the rated RCCT 50Hz signal. This must be taken into consideration for the selection of an appropriate modulation frequency.

The upper graph of Figure 8.8 shows the spectrum of the corrected signal. The rated RCCT 50Hz signal spectrum is evident while the rest of the frequency components correspond to the spikes in the time domain. The spikes have a fundamental frequency of 2.5Hz, equivalent to the modulation frequency, and frequency components on each odd multiple of it. This modulation frequency was specifically selected in order for its harmonics not to interfere with the 50Hz rated signal spectrum.

8.2.4 Evaluation

An FPGA based platform was developed in parallel to the work presented here. Both platforms, virtual and real, used the same embedded software, with the exception of some hardware-dependent drivers. Figure 8.8 shows the comparison between the corrected signals spectra of the simulation and the implementation results. The main difference between them lies on the noise sources. In the virtual platform, no white noise sources were introduced in the AMS model, which explains the defined spectrum shapes in comparison to the implementation results. The results were encouraging since both platforms were functionally equivalent, which validates the correctness of our simulation models and the importance of performing multi-domain simulations for verification purposes.

The results form this case study show that the dynamic verification of embedded systems in the industrial automation domain can be complemented by the use of multi-domain virtual platforms. While this is still a current research topic and the integration of virtual platforms in development processes is still experimental in the industrial automation domain, first results indicate that this approach can improve the way engineers develop and verify systems using multi-domain simulation models.

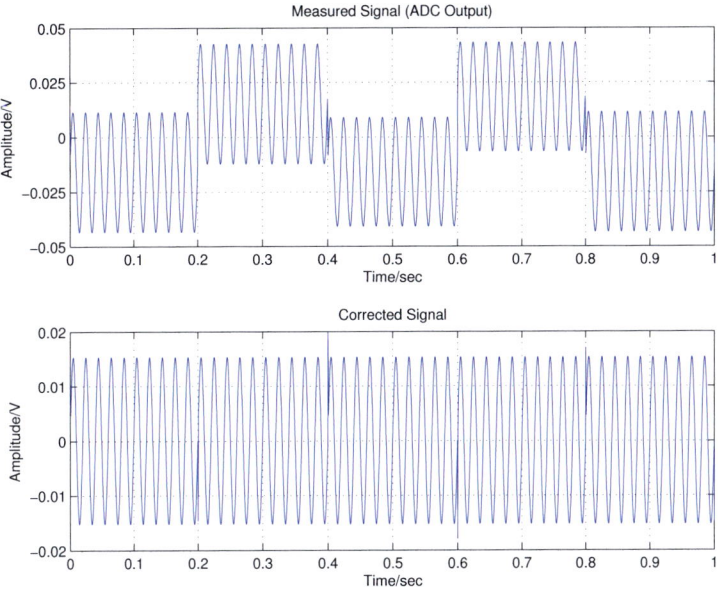

Figure 8.7: Simulation data for measured and corrected signals

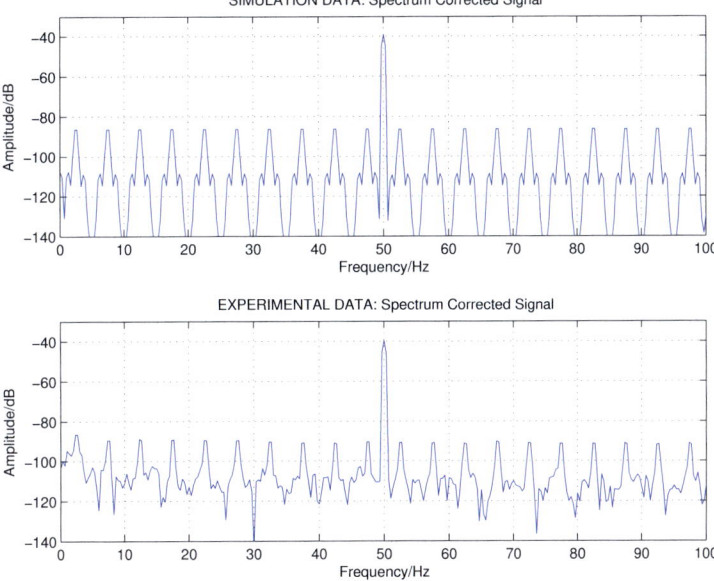

Figure 8.8: Simulation and experimental data for the corrected signal spectrum

9

Conclusions and Outlook

9.1 Conclusions

This dissertation described a virtual prototyping methodology for the design and verification of heterogeneous embedded systems. Its goal is to provide multidisciplinary team members enhanced verification capabilities to identify and solve design problems during early development stages. This is possible by coupling the execution of different simulators, each one responsible for obtaining the behavior of part of a system. The combined execution of simulators can help increase the understanding of interdependencies between different system components. This eventually helps increase the confidence in the correctness of a design, thereby reducing risks in a project and leading to hardware prototypes and experimental setups that are built right the first time.

The contribution to the state-of-the-art is a design and verification methodology that combines digital systems, analog and mixed-signal systems and multi-domain physical systems for the creation of virtual prototypes that are able to emulate (mimic) the behavior of real hardware prototypes and experimental setups. Related work on this topic had not fully addressed issues such as: (1) the use of virtual prototypes for supporting various stages of the development life-cycle of heterogeneous embedded systems, (2) tooling integration for model exchange and (3) the reuse of available device firmware (embedded software code).

The milestones achieved in this dissertation together with their respective publications are summarized as follows:

- *A problem-oriented verification methodology* [91].- it proposes a set of abstraction layers for the construction of virtual prototypes. The most adequate abstraction can be selected according to the development stage and to particular verification goals, allowing for top-down or bottom-up verification approaches. This enables the verification of a design in various stages to evaluate the impact that different design decisions may have on it. Most importantly, it enables to detect and solve design problems before they propagate into further development stages.

- *A set of modeling guidelines* [89, 92].- intended to decrease the implementation effort of the proposed design methodology. The guidelines provide a set of rules for the construction of consistent and meaningful virtual prototypes. They are intended to ease the creation of virtual prototypes and to increases the reusability of designs.

- *A multi-domain simulation framework* [90, 92].- it is the result of coupling specialized simulation tools for HW/SW co-design of embedded systems and simulation tools for multi-domain physical systems. The coupling is done with a co-simulation scheme that defines the control and communication semantics for the coupled execution of discrete-event and continuous-time simulators. The framework currently implements the co-simulation between SystemC/Simulink and SystemC/VHDL-AMS for the creation of virtual prototypes. It does not affect the usability of the models involved (no special changes needed) and does not interfere with their inherent models of computation (discrete-event or continuous-time).

The modeling languages and simulation tools used in this work are in accordance to best-practices in the industrial automation. In the case of physical domain modeling, MATLAB/Simulink is already a widely accepted and used tool among control engineers and physicists, whereas VHDL-AMS is slowly becoming accepted by a specialized group of users. In the case of digital domain modeling, SystemC is gaining acceptance in this field, especially among software engineers. This claim is supported by the industrial case study presented in this work and by related work in the industrial automation domain [101, 113, 133].

This dissertation is intended to serve as starting platform for further research on the use of virtual prototypes in the development flow of industrial devices. While this is still a current research topic and the integration of virtual prototypes in development processes is still experimental in the industrial automation domain, first results indicate that this approach can improve the way engineers design and verify heterogeneous embedded systems.

9.2 Outlook

The topics presented ahead have been identified as further research areas which can benefit from the results obtained in this dissertation:

1. *Robustness testing.*- Assess the reliability of embedded systems by automated fault injection testing in a virtual prototype. Quantize the influence of tolerances in mechanical, pneumatic, electric and electronic components in a design.

2. *Real-time interfacing capabilities.*- Provide real-time interfacing capabilities to virtual prototypes for controlling a real environment and for communicating with real industrial networks.

3. *Timing and power annotation.*- Annotation of timing and power figures from a real platform into a virtual prototype. This can help estimate with a considerable accuracy the power consumption of devices.

4. *Industrial automation networks .*- Simulation of industrial automation networks relying on different physical mediums (wired and non-wired) for the verification of novel distributed control applications.

5. *Factory acceptance tests .*- Simulation of industrial devices and industrial networks in a large scale (thousands of interconnected devices). Perform factory acceptance tests of devices and their industrial processes in a virtual environment. This can save time and resources during the commissioning phase of industrial devices.

Acronyms

ADC	Analog to Digital Converter
AFE	Analog Front-End
AMS	Analog and Mixed-Signal
API	Application Programming Interface
CPS	Cyber-Physical System
CT	Continuous Time
DAC	Digital to Analog Converter
DAE	Differentia Algebraic Equation
DCS	Distributed Control Systems
DE	Discrete Event
EDA	Electronic Design Automation
ELN	Electrical Linear Networks
ERP	Enterprise Resource Planning
FMI	Functional Mock-up Interface
FSM	Finite State Machine
HART	Highway Addressable Remote Transducer
HDL	Hardware Description Language
HdS	Hardware Dependent Software

HMI	Human Machine Interface
HVAC	Heating, Ventilation and Air Conditioning
HW	Hardware
HW/SW	Hardware/Software
I/O	Input/Output
IC	Integrated Circuit
IDE	Integrated Development Environment
IED	Intelligent Electronic Device
IPC	Instructions Per Cycle
ISR	Interrupt Service Routine
ISS	Instruction Set Simulator
LSF	Linear Signal Flow
MES	Manufacturing Execution Systems
MoC	Model of Computation
MPSoC	Multi-processor System on Chip
ODE	Ordinary Differential Equation
OVP	Open Virtual Platforms
PE	Processing Element
PER	Peripheral
PID	Proportional Integral Derivative
PLC	Programmable Logic Controller
RTL	Register Transfer Level
RTOS	Real-Time Operating System
SCADA	Supervisory Control and Data Acquisition

SDF	Synchronous Data Flow
SNR	Signal-to-Noise Ratio
SoC	System on Chip
SW	Software
TDF	Timed Data Flow
TLM	Transaction Level Modeling
VIC	Vector Interrupt Controller
VP	Virtual Prototype

Bibliography

[1] Accellera Systems Initiative. *www.accellera.org*.

[2] Boost C++ Libraries. *www.boost.org*.

[3] ABB AG. Freelance 800F The compact control system, 2009.

[4] AbsInt Angewandte Informatik GmbH. aiT Worst-/case Execution Time Analyzers. *www.absint.com/ait*.

[5] S. Adhikari and C. Grimm. Modeling Switched Capacitor Sigma Delta Modulator Nonidealities in SystemC-AMS. In *Proceedings of the 2010 Forum on specification & Design Languages*, pages 216–221, 2010.

[6] American Institute of Aeronautics and Astronautics Staf (AAIA). *Guide for the Verification and Validation of Computational Fluid Dynamics Simulations*. American Institute of Aeronautics & Astronautics, 1998.

[7] ANSYS Inc. ANSYS Simplorer. *www.ansys.com/Products/Simulation+Technology/Electromagnetics/Electromechanical+Design/ANSYS+Simplorer*.

[8] ARM Ltd. uVision IDE. *www.keil.com/uvision*.

[9] P. J. Ashenden, G. D. Peterson, and D. A. Teegarden. *The System Designer's Guide to VHDL-AMS: Analog, Mixed-Signal, and Mixed-Technology Modeling*. Morgan Kaufmann, 2002.

[10] F. Balarin, Y. Watanabe, H. Hsieh, L. Lavagno, C. Passerone, and A. Sangiovanni-Vincentelli. Metropolis: an integrated electronic system design environment. *Computer Journal of the IEEE Computer Society*, 36(4):45–52, Apr. 2003.

[11] M. Barnasconi. SystemC AMS Extensions: Solving the Need for Speed. Technical report, DAC.COM Knowledge Center Article, 2010.

[12] G. Behrmann, A. David, and K. Larsen. A Tutorial on Uppaal. In *Formal Methods for the Design of Real-Time Systems*, volume 3185 of *Lecture Notes in Computer Science*, pages 33–35. Springer Berlin / Heidelberg, 2004.

[13] F. Bellard. QEMU, a fast and portable dynamic translator. *USENIX Annual Technical Conference*, page 41, 2005.

[14] L. Benini, D. Bertozzi, D. Bruni, N. Drago, F. Fummi, and M. Poncino. SystemC cosimulation and emulation of multiprocessor SoC designs. *IEEE Computer Society*, 36(4):53–59, Apr. 2003.

[15] J. Bennett. Building a Loosely Timed SoC Model with OSCI TLM 2.0. A Case Study Using an Open Source ISS and Linux 2.6 Kernel. Technical Report 2, Embecosm, 2010.

[16] J. Berge. *Introduction to Fieldbuses for Process Control*. ISA - The Instrumentation, Systems, and Automation Society, 2002.

[17] D. C. Black, J. Donovan, B. Bunton, and A. Keist. *SystemC: From the ground up*. Springer Verlag, 2009.

[18] H. I. Blanchard. Emulation and cross-development for PowerPC, Jan. 2005. *www.ibm.com/developerworks/library/pa-emulation.html*.

[19] R. Bolton and S. Tyler. PQLI Engineering Controls and Automation Strategy. *Journal of Pharmaceutical Innovation*, 3(2):88–94, 2008.

[20] J.-F. Borland, C. Thibeault, and Z. Zilic. Using Matlab and Simulink in SystemC verification environment. In *Proceedings of Design and Verification Conference, DVCon05*, Dec. 2005.

[21] F. Bouchhima, G. Nicolescu, E. M. Aboulhamid, and M. Abid. Generic discrete-continuous simulation model for accurate validation in heterogeneous systems design. *Microelectronics Journal*, 38(6-7):805–815, June 2007.

[22] K.-P. Brand. The concept of IEC 61850. In *ABB Review Special Report IEC 61850*, pages 7–12. ABB Group R&D and Technology, 2010.

[23] M. Branicky. Introduction to Hybrid Systems. In *Handbook of Networked and Embedded Control Systems*, Control Engineering, pages 91–116. Birkhäuser Boston, 2005.

[24] Cadence Design Systems Inc. Virtual System Platform. *www.cadence.com/products/sd/virtual_system.*

[25] L. Cai and D. Gajski. Transaction Level Modeling: an overview. In *IEEE/ACM/IFIP International Conference on Hardware/ Software Codesign and Systems Synthesis*, pages 19–24. ACM, 2003.

[26] K. Caluwaerts and D. Galayko. SystemC-AMS modeling of an electromechanical harvester of vibration energy. In *2008 Forum on Specification, Verification and Design Languages*, pages 99–104. IEEE, Sept. 2008.

[27] Carbon Design Systems Inc. Carbon ARM Model Library. *www.carbondesignsystems.com.*

[28] Center for Embedded Comptuer Systems (CECS). *Embedded Systems Environment.* University of California, Irvine, 2010. *www.cecs.uci.edu/~ese.*

[29] A. Cervin and K.-E. Å rzén. TrueTime: Simulation Tool for Performance Analysis of Real-Time Embedded Systems. In *Model-Based Design for Embedded Systems*, chapter 6. CRC Press, Nov. 2009.

[30] E. Christen and K. Bakalar. VHDL-AMS-a hardware description language for analog and mixed-signal applications. In *IEEE Transactions on Circuits and Systems II: Analog and Digital Signal Processing*, volume 46, pages 1263–1272, 1999.

[31] E. Clarke, O. Grumberg, S. Jha, Y. Lu, and H. Veith. Counterexample-guided abstraction refinement for symbolic model checking. *Journal of the ACM*, 50(5): 752–794, Sept. 2003.

[32] E. M. Clarke and E. A. Emerson. Design and Synthesis of Synchronization Skeletons Using Branching-Time Temporal Logic. In *Logic of Programs, Workshop*, pages 52–71, London, UK, 1981. Springer-Verlag.

[33] E. M. Clarke and B.-H. Schlingloff. Model Checking. In *Handbook of Automated Reasoning*, pages 1635–1790. Elsevier and MIT Press, 2001.

[34] A. Clouard, K. Jain, F. Ghenassia, L. Maillet-Contoz, and J.-P. Strassen. Using transactional level models in a SoC design flow. In *SystemC: Methodologies and Applications*, pages 29–63. Kluwer Academic Publishers, Norwell, MA, USA, 2003.

[35] P. Coussy and A. Morawiec. *High-Level Synthesis: from Algorithm to Digital Circuit.* Springer, 2008.

[36] A. Davare, D. Densmore, T. Meyerowitz, A. Pinto, A. Sangiovanni-Vincentelli, G. Yang, H. Zeng, and Q. Zhu. A Next-Generation Design Framework for Platform-based Design. In *Proceedings of Design and Verification Conference, DVCon07*, 2007.

[37] Delta V Software. RCF - Remote Call Framework. *www.deltavsoft.com*.

[38] P. Derler, E. A. Lee, and A. S. Vincentelli. Modeling Cyber-Physical Systems. *Proceedings of the IEEE*, 100(1):13–28, Jan. 2012.

[39] Deutsches Institut für Normung. DIN V 19222: Leittechnik - Begriffe. Technical report, Beuth, Berlin, 2001.

[40] Dolphin Integration. SMASH Mixed-Signal Simulator. *www.dolphin.fr/medal/products/smash/smash_overview.php*.

[41] R. Domer, A. Gerstlauer, and W. Muller. Introduction to Hardware-dependent Software design. In *2009 Asia and South Pacific Design Automation Conference*, pages 290–292. IEEE, Jan. 2009.

[42] A. Donlin. Transaction level modeling: flows and use models. In *Proceedings of the 2nd IEEE/ACM/IFIP international conference on Hardware/software codesign and system synthesis*, CODES+ISSS '04, pages 75–80, New York, NY, USA, 2004.

[43] K. Ehinger, D. Flach, L. Gellrich, E. Horlebein, R. Huck, H. Ilgner, T. Kayser, H. Müller, H. Schädlich, A. Schüssler, and U. Staab. *Praxis der industriellen Temperaturmessung*. ABB Automation Products, 2008.

[44] J. Eker, J. Janneck, E. A. Lee, J. Liu, X. Liu, J. Ludvig, S. Sachs, and Y. Xiong. Taming heterogeneity - the Ptolemy approach. *Proceedings of the IEEE*, 91(1):127–144, 2003.

[45] J. Engblom, D. Aarno, and B. Werner. Full-System Simulation from Embedded to High-Performance Systems. *Processor and System-on-Chip Simulation*, 2010.

[46] Fraunhofer-Gesellschaft. SystemC-AMS PoC Beta 2. *systemc-ams.eas.iis.fraunhofer.de*.

[47] D. Gajski and R. Kuhn. Guest Editors' Introduction: New VLSI Tools. *Computer Journal of the IEEE Computer Society*, 16(12):11–14, Dec. 1983.

[48] D. D. Gajski, J. Zhu, R. Domer, A. Gerstlauer, and S. Zhao. *SpecC: Specification Language and Methodology*. Springer, 1 edition, 2000.

[49] D. D. Gajski, S. Abdi, A. Gerstlauer, and G. Schirner. *Embedded System Design: Modeling, Synthesis and Verification.* Springer, 2009.

[50] E. Gamma, R. Helm, R. Johnson, and J. Vlissides. *Design Patterns.* Addison-Wesley, Boston, MA, 1995.

[51] L. Gheorghe, G. Nicolescu, and H. Boucheneb. Generic Methodology for the Design of Continuous/Discrete Co-Simulation Tools. In *Model-Based Design for Embedded Systems*, chapter 16. CRC Press, 2009.

[52] G. Giorgidze. *FIRST-CLASS MODELS On a Noncausal Language for Higher-order and Structurally Dynamic Modelling and Simulation.* PhD thesis, The University of Nottingham, 2011.

[53] R. Görgen, F. Voit, and A. Rettberg. SystemC-Based Emulation of Hardware Platforms in a Physical Environment. In *QVVP Workshop at DATE 2012*, 2012.

[54] C. Grimm, W. Heupke, and K. Waldschmidt. Refinement of Mixed-Signal Systems with Affine Arithmetic. In *Design Automation &Test in Europe*, DATE '04, Washington, DC, USA, 2004. IEEE Computer Society.

[55] T. Grötker, S. Liao, G. Martin, and S. Swan. *System Design with SystemC.* Kluwer Academic Publishers, 2002.

[56] J. Hansson and S. Bollmeyer. When two become one. In *ABB Review Special Report IEC 61850*, pages 42–46. ABB Group R&D and Technology, Aug. 2010.

[57] D. Harel and A. Pnueli. On the development of reactive systems. In *Logics and models of concurrent systems*, pages 477–498. Springer-Verlag New York, Inc., New York, NY, USA, 1985.

[58] HART Communication Foundation. FSK Physical Layer Test Specification. Technical report, 1999.

[59] P. A. Hartmann, P. Reinkemeier, A. Rettberg, and W. Nebel. Modelling control systems in SystemC AMS - Benefits and limitations. In *2009 IEEE International SOC Conference (SOCC)*, pages 263–266. IEEE, Sept. 2009.

[60] W. Hassairi, M. Bousselmi, M. Abid, and C. V. Sakuyama. Using matlab and Simulink in SystemC verification environment By JPEG algorithm. In *2009 16th IEEE International Conference on Electronics, Circuits and Systems - (ICECS 2009)*, pages 912–915. IEEE, Dec. 2009.

[61] C. Haubelt, T. Schlichter, J. Keinert, and M. Meredith. *SystemCoDesigner: Automatic Design Space Exploration and Rapid Prototyping from Behavioral Models*. ACM Press, New York, NY, USA, 2008.

[62] C. Helmstetter, V. Joloboff, and H. Xiao. SimSoC: A full system simulation software for embedded systems. In *2009 International Workshop on Open-source Software for Scientific Computation (OSSC-2009)*, page 7 p., Sept. 2009.

[63] P. Herber. *A Framework for Automated HW / SW Co-Verification of SystemC Designs using Timed Automata*. Dissertation, Technischen Universität Berlin, 2010.

[64] W. Heupke, C. Grimm, and K. Waldschmidt. Modeling Uncertainty in Nonlinear Systems with Affine Arithmetic. In *Advances in Specification and Design Languages for SoC*, pages 198 – 213. Springer-Verlag, 2006.

[65] G. Holzmann. The model checker SPIN. *IEEE Transactions on Software Engineering*, 23(5):279–295, May 1997.

[66] K. Hylla, J.-H. Oetjens, and W. Nebel. Using SystemC for an extended MATLAB/Simulink verification flow. In *2008 Forum on Specification, Verification and Design Languages*, pages 221–226. IEEE, Sept. 2008.

[67] IAR Systems. IAR Embedded Workbench. *www.iar.com*.

[68] IEEE Computer Society. *1666-2005: IEEE Standard for SystemC Language Reference Manual*. 2006.

[69] IEEE Computer Society. 1076.1-2009 - Behavioural languages - Part 6: VHDL Analog and Mixed-Signal Extensions. 2009.

[70] IEEE Computer Society. *1666-2011: IEEE Standard for SystemC Language Reference Manual*. 2011.

[71] IEEE Computer Society and IEEE Standards Association Corporate Advisory Group. *1685-2009: IEEE Standard for IP-XACT, Standard Structure for Packaging, Integrating, and Reusing IP within Tool Flows*. 2009.

[72] IEEE Standards Association. *1012-2004: IEEE Standard for Software Verification and Validation*. 2004.

[73] Imperas. OVP Open Virtual Platforms. *www.ovpworld.org*.

[74] ISA International Society of Automation. *ISA-95 : Enterprise Control Systems*.

[75] G. Karsai and J. Sztipanovits. Model-Integrated Development of Cyber-Physical Systems. In *Software Technologies for Embedded and Ubiquitous Systems*, volume 5287 of *Lecture Notes in Computer Science*, pages 46–54. Springer Berlin / Heidelberg, 2008.

[76] K. Keutzer, A. Newton, J. Rabaey, and A. Sangiovanni-Vincentelli. System-level design: orthogonalization of concerns and platform-based design. In *IEEE Transactions on Computer-Aided Design of Integrated Circuits and Systems*, volume 19, pages 1523–1543, 2000.

[77] T. Kirchner, N. Bannow, and C. Grimm. Analogue mixed signal simulation using spice and SystemC. In *Design, Automation & Test in Europe Conference & Exhibition, 2009. DATE '09.*, pages 284–287, 2009.

[78] T. Kirchner, N. Bannow, and C. Grimm. Mixed Signal Simulation with SystemC and Saber. In *Proceedings of the 2010 Forum on specification & Design Languages*, pages 111–116. ECSI, Electronic Chips & Systems design Initiative, 2010.

[79] S. Kundu, M. Ganai, and R. Gupta. Partial order reduction for scalable testing of systemC TLM designs. In *Proceedings of the 45th annual conference on Design automation - DAC '08*, page 936, New York, NY, USA, 2008. ACM Press.

[80] L. Lavagno and C. Passerone. Desing of Embedded Systems. In *Embedded Systems Handbook*, chapter 3. 2006.

[81] E. Lee and D. Messerschmitt. Synchronous data flow. *Proceedings of the IEEE*, 75 (9):1235–1245, 1987.

[82] E. A. Lee. Cyber-Physical Systems -Are Computing Foundations Adequate? In *NSF Workshop On Cyber-Physical Systems: Research Motivation, Techniques and Roadmap*, 2006.

[83] E. A. Lee and S. A. Seshia. *Introduction to Embedded Systems, A Cyber-Physical Systems Approach.* 2011.

[84] E. A. Lee and S. Tripakis. Modal Models in Ptolemy. In *Proceedings of 3rd International Workshop on Equation-Based Object-Oriented Modeling Languages and Tools (EOOLT 2010)*, pages 1–11, Oct. 2010.

[85] J.-K. Lee, M.-W. Lee, and S.-D. Chi. DEVS/HLA-Based Modeling and Simulation for Intelligent Transportation Systems. *SIMULATION*, 79(8):423–439, Aug. 2003.

[86] Maplesoft division of Waterloo Maple Inc. MapleSim: High-Perfromance Physical Modeling and Simulation. *www.maplesoft.com/products/maplesim*.

[87] D. A. Mathaikutty, H. D. Patel, S. K. Shukla, and A. Jantsch. SML-Sys: a functional framework with multiple models of computation for modeling heterogeneous system. *Design Automation for Embedded Systems*, 12(1-2):1–30, Mar. 2008.

[88] F. Mendoza. SmartFD Project - Annual Report, 2010.

[89] F. Mendoza and J. Becker. Domain Specific Virtual Platforms. In *QVVP Workshop from the Design Automation &Test in Europe (DATE) Conference*, 2012.

[90] F. Mendoza, C. Kollner, J. Becker, and K. D. Muller-Glaser. An automated approach to SystemC/Simulink co-simulation. In *2011 22nd IEEE International Symposium on Rapid System Prototyping*, pages 135–141. IEEE, May 2011.

[91] F. Mendoza, P. Nenninger, M. Ruppert, and J. Becker. Scalable problem-oriented approach for dynamic verification of embedded systems. In *IFAC Conference on Embedded Systems, Computational Intellingence and Telematics in Control*, pages 224–229. IFAC, 2012.

[92] F. Mendoza, J. Pascal, P. Nenninger, and J. Becker. Framework for Dynamic Verification of Multi- Domain Virtual Platforms in Industrial Automation. In *IEEE 10th International Conference on Industrial Informatics*, 2012.

[93] Mentor Graphics. SystemVision. *www.mentor.com/products/sm/system_integration_simulation_analysis/systemvision*.

[94] Mirabilis Design Inc. VisualSim. *www.mirabilisdesign.com/Pages/Product/mdi_products.htm*.

[95] P. Mittelstaedt and P. Weingartner. *Laws of nature*. Springer Verlag, 2005.

[96] MLDesign Technologies Inc. MLDesigner. *www.mldesigner.com/mldesigner*.

[97] Modelica. *A Unified Object-Oriented Language for Physical Systems Modeling : Language Specification Version 3.2*. The Modelica Association, 2010. *https://www.modelica.org/documents/ModelicaSpec32.pdf*.

[98] MODELISAR. Functional Mock-up Interface for Model Exchange and Co-Simulation, 2012. *www.fmi-standard.org*.

[99] M. Montón. *Checkpointing for Virtual Platforms*. Phd thesis, Autonomous University of Barcelona, 2010.

[100] P. Nenninger, T. Merlin, D. John, and F. Kantz. Komponentenbasierte Entwicklung von Firmware für Sensorsysteme in der industriellen Praxis. In *Evolutionäre Software- und Systementwicklung - Methoden und Erfahrungen*, 2011.

[101] P. Nenninger, T. Ruschival, and G. L. Madonna. Design and Implementation of a Master-Slave Communication Protocol for Embedded Systems Using SystemC. In *IFAC Conference on Embedded Systems, Computational Intellingence and Telematics in Control*. IFAC, 2012.

[102] A. Nohl, G. Braun, O. Schliebusch, R. Leupers, H. Meyr, and A. Hoffmann. A universal technique for fast and flexible instruction-set architecture simulation. In *Proceedings 2002 Design Automation Conference*, pages 22–27. ACM, June 2002.

[103] Object Management Group. OMG's MetaObject Facility. *www.omg.org/mof*.

[104] OFFIS - Institute for Information Technology. OFFIS SimLink: Open Virtual Platform - Matlab/Simulink co-simulation. *system-synthesis.org/offissimlink*.

[105] OSCI AMS Working Group. *SystemC AMS extensions User's Guide*. Release 1.0, 2010. *www.accellera.org*.

[106] OSCI AMS Working Group. *Standard SystemC AMS extensions Language Reference Manual*. Release 1.0, 2010. *www.accellera.org*.

[107] J. Pascal, R. Bloch, S. Isler, and L. Georges. Electronic Front End for Rogowski Coil Current Transducers with Online Accuracy Self Monitoring. In *IEEE International Conference on Industrial Technology*, 2012.

[108] H. D. Patel and S. K. Shukla. Towards a heterogeneous simulation kernel for system level models. In *Proceedins of the 14th ACM Great Lakes symposium on VLSI - GLSVLSI '04*, page 248, New York, New York, USA, 2004. ACM Press.

[109] C. L. Phillips and R. D. Harbor. *Feedback Control Systems*. Prentice Hall, second edition, 1991.

[110] N. Pouillon, A. Becoulet, A. V. D. Mello, F. Pecheux, and A. Greiner. A Generic Instruction Set Simulator API for Timed and Untimed Simulation and Debug of MP2-SoCs. In *2009 IEEE/IFIP International Symposium on Rapid System Prototyping*, pages 116–122. Ieee, June 2009.

[111] M. Reshadi, P. Mishra, and N. Dutt. Instruction set compiled simulation. In *Proceedings of the 40th conference on Design automation - DAC '03*, page 758, New York, New York, USA, June 2003. ACM Press.

[112] S. Rigo, G. Araujo, M. Bartholomeu, and R. Azevedo. ArchC: A SystemC-Based Architecture Description Language. In *16th Symposium on Computer Architecture and High Performance Computing*, pages 66–73. IEEE, 2004.

[113] M. Ruppert. *Evaluation of SystemC Processor Models in the Development Process of Industrial Instruments*. Master thesis, Hochschule Darmstadt, 2011.

[114] I. Sander and A. Jantsch. System Modeling and Transformational Design Refinement in ForSyDe. *IEEE Transactions on Computer-Aided Design of Integrated Circuits and Systems*, 23(1):17–32, Jan. 2004.

[115] S. Schlesinger. Terminology for model credibility. *SIMULATION*, 32(3):103–104, Mar. 1979.

[116] J. Schnerr, O. Bringmann, M. Krause, A. Viehl, and W. Rosentiel. SystemC-Based Performance Analysis of Embedded Systems. In *Model-Based Design for Embedded Systems (Computational Analysis, Synthesis, and Design of Dynamic Systems)*, chapter 2, page 766. 2009.

[117] L. F. Shampine and M. W. Reichelt. The MATLAB ODE Suite. *SIAM Journal on Scientific Computing*, 18(1):1, 1997.

[118] SimpleScalar LLC. SimpleScalar. *www.simplescalar.com*.

[119] S. Sutherland, S. Davidmann, and P. Flake. *SystemVerilog for Design: A guide to using SystemVerilog for hardware design and modeling*. Springer-Verlag New York Inc, 2006.

[120] S. Swan. SystemC transaction level models and RTL verification. In *2006 43rd ACM/IEEE Design Automation Conference*, pages 90–92. Ieee, 2006.

[121] Synopsys Inc. CoMET-METeor, . *www.synopsys.com/Systems/VirtualPrototyping/Pages/CoMET-METeor.aspx*.

[122] Synopsys Inc. Platform Architect, . *www.synopsys.com/SYSTEMS/ARCHITECTUREDESIGN/Pages/PlatformArchitect.aspx*.

[123] Synopsys Inc. Saber, . *www.synopsys.com/systems/saber*.

[124] Synopsys Inc. Synopsys Virtual Prototyping, . *www.synopsys.com/Systems/VirtualPrototyping*.

[125] Y. Tanurhan. *Zum kooperativen Entwurf von eingebetteten Echtzeitsystemen*. Dissertation, Universität Karlsruhe, 1998.

[126] Texas Instruments Incorporated. Code Composer Studio IDE. *www.ti.com/tool/ccstudio*.

[127] B. H. Thacker, S. W. Doebling, F. M. Hemez, M. C. Anderson, J. E. Pepin, and E. A. Rodriguez. *Concepts of Model Verification and Validation*. Los Alamos National Lab., NM., 2004.

[128] The Mathworks Inc. Simscape: Model and simulate mulidomain physical systems, . *www.mathworks.de/products/simscape*.

[129] The Mathworks Inc. Simulink documentation, . *www.mathworks.de/help/toolbox/simulink*.

[130] The Mathworks Inc. Simulink Coder, . *www.mathworks.de/products/simulink-coder*.

[131] C. Traulsen, J. Cornet, M. Moy, and F. Maraninchi. A SystemC/TLM semantics in Promela and its possible applications. In *14th Workshop on Model Checking Software SPIN*, July 2007.

[132] A. Vachoux, C. Grimm, and K. Einwich. Towards Analog and Mixed-Signal SOC Design with SystemC-AMS. In *Second IEEE International Workshop on Electronic Design, Test and Applications (DELTA)*, 2004.

[133] R. Valentina, M. Ruppert, P. Nenninger, and F. Mendoza. Human Machine Interface for Virtual Prototyping of Industrial Instruments. In *IEEE 11th International Conference on Industrial Informatics*, 2013.

[134] M. Verhoef. *Modeling and Validating Distributed Embedded Real-Time Control Systems*. Phd thesis, Radboud University Nijmegen, 2008.

[135] G. A. Wainer. *Discrete-Event Modeling and Simulation: A Practitioner's Approach*. Computational analysis, synthesis, and design of dynamic models series. CRC Press, 2009.

[136] M. Wetter. Co-simulation of building energy and control systems with the Building Controls Virtual Test Bed. *Journal of Building Performance Simulation*, 4(3):185–203, Sept. 2011.

[137] Xilinx Inc. Vivado Design Suite. *www.xilinx.com/products/design-tools/vivado/index.htm.*

[138] B. P. Zeigler, H. Praehofer, and T. G. Kim. *Theory of modeling and simulation,* volume 100. Academic Press New York, 2000.